The Cathedral Dedicated to the Apostle, St. Peter

St. Peter Cathedral
Marquette, MI

Written by
Deacon Scott A. Jamieson

The Cathedral Dedicated to the Apostle, St. Peter

by Deacon Scott A. Jamieson

Published by The Bishop Baraga Association, Marquette, Michigan

Book Design by The Bishop Baraga Association

Hardcover ISBN: 9798218544225

Paperback ISBN: 9798218544133

Front Cover photography by James Howe

Back Cover photography by Lenora McKeen, Bishop Baraga Association

About the Author

Scott Jamieson, a lifelong Michigander, moved to Marquette with his wife, Claudia, in 1977 to open his orthodontic practice in which he was involved until 2020 when his son took over. Scott and Claudia became members of St. Peter Cathedral when they arrived in Marquette.

Despite having earned a D.D.S and a M.S. degree, Scott found himself with an incomplete Bachelor's degree. To complete the final degree requirement, Northern Michigan University History Professor and fellow parishioner, Dr. Barry Knight, suggested that he document the history of St. Peter Cathedral. While maintaining his orthodontic practice full-time and raising two of his four children, Scott completed, The Cathedral Dedicated to the Apostle, St. Peter, in 1982.

Scott and Claudia's four children were baptized in St. Peter Cathedral. He was ordained to the Diaconate in 1996 by Bishop James Garland, at which time Scott was assigned to the Cathedral where he served for 14 years. He was then assigned to St. Louis the King parish where he continues to serve. Scott served as the Director of the Diaconate for the Diocese of Marquette for many years. Scott and Claudia are Knight and Lady of the Holy Sepulchre. In addition, he is also a member of is the Knights of Columbus and a proud supporter of the Bishop Baraga Association.

What started as an assignment to fulfill his degree requirement soon became a passion of his faith. A tour guide of St. Peter Cathedral evolved from the book and is available through the Bishop Baraga Association.

THE CATHEDRAL DEDICATED TO THE APOSTLE, ST. PETER

St. Peter Cathedral
Marquette, Michigan

In fulfillment of the requirements
History # 498
Northern Michigan University
Marquette, Michigan

by

Scott Allan Jamieson, D.D.S, M.S.
Marquette, Michigan
February, 1982

Revised October, 2024 by the author

<u>CONTENTS</u>

BISHOPS OF THE SAULT STE. MARIE AND MARQUETTE DIOCESE

		Installation	Retirement/Transfer
*(1)	Bishop Frederic Ireneus Baraga	Nov. 1, 1853 -	Jan. 19, 1868
*(2)	Bishop Ignatius Mrak	Feb. 7, 1869 -	Apr. 28, 1879
*(3)	Bishop John Vertin	Sept. 14, 1879 -	Feb. 26, 1899
*(4)	Bishop Frederick Eis	Aug. 24, 1899 -	July 8, 1922
*(5)	Bishop Paul Joseph Nussbaum	Feb. 5, 1923 -	June 24, 1935
*(6)	Bishop Joseph Casimir Plagens	Jan. 29, 1936 -	Dec. 14, 1940
*(7)	Bishop Francis Joseph Magner	Nov. 20, 1941 -	June 13, 1947
*(8)	Bishop Thomas Lawrence Noa	Sept. 24, 1947 -	Mar. 25, 1968
+*(9)	Bishop Charles Alexander Salatka Installed as Archbishop of Oklahoma City, Oklahoma	Mar. 25, 1968 -	Sept. 27, 1977 Dec. 15, 1977
*(10)	Bishop Mark Francis Schmitt	May 8, 1978 -	Oct. 6, 1992
(11)	Bishop James Henry Garland	Nov. 11, 1992 -	Dec. 12, 2005
+(12)	Bishop Alexander King Sample Installed as Archbishop of Portland in Oregon	Jan. 25, 2006 -	Jan. 29, 2013 Apr. 2, 2013
(13)	Bishop John Francis Doerfler	Feb. 11, 2014 -	Present

* Deceased
\+ Archbishop

PASTORS AND/OR RECTORS OF ST. PETER CATHEDRAL

*Fr. Sebastian   Duroc

*Fr. Henry L. Thiele

*Fr. Edward Jacker

*Fr. Edmond   Walsh

*Fr. Mangee

*Fr. Martin Eis

*Fr. John   Brown

*Fr. Hugh   McDavitt

*Fr. Oliver Comtois

*Fr. H.J. Rousseau

*Fr. A. 0. Pellisson

*Fr. T. A. Crantonberg

*Fr. John   C.   Henry

*Fr. John   C. Kenny

*Fr. A. W.   Geers

*Fr. Charles   Drees

*Fr. Martin Keough

*Fr. M. McClay

*Fr. A. Panelle

*Fr. F. X. Becker

*Fr. T. A. Magerust

*Fr. Villian Haas

*Fr. Joseph   Beron

*Fr. Matthew Lyons

*Fr. Fabian Marceau

*Fr. F. X. Winniger, S. J.

*Fr. Thomas   Turner

*Fr. Augustine Boyer, O.S.F.

*Fr. J.E. Struif

*Fr. Philip   Kummert
*Fr. Ignatius Balluff

*Fr. J. A. Keul

*Fr. Joseph   Langan

*Fr. James   Miller

*Fr. N. H. Nosbisch

*Fr. Adam   Doser

*Fr. Joseph G. Pinten

*Fr. Henry A. Buchholtz

*Msgr. John T. Holland

*Fr. Glen Sanford

*Msgr. Nolan B. McKevitt

*Msgr. Louis C. Cappo

**Msgr. Michael Steber

***Fr. Brandon Oman

*   Deceased
** Retired
*** Present

A CONCISE HISTORY OF   ST. PETER CATHEDRAL

Saint Peter's was founded as a parish in the Summer of 1853 when a Jesuit priest, Father Menet, S.J., arrived to celebrate Mass in Marquette and serve the Catholic population. This first Mass was celebrated in a log cabin which was located on what is presently called Spring Street. Thereafter, on occasion, the city was visited by the Jesuits stationed at Sault Ste. Marie.

On October 12, 1853, Bishop Frederic Baraga visited the city, confirmed 30 persons, then selected the site for the construction of a new church. This site is where the present Cathedral of St. Peter's is now standing, the corner of Baraga Avenue and Fourth Street.

The first resident priest, Father Sebastian Duroc, was instructed by Bishop Baraga to leave Mackinac Island in the late Fall of 1856 and proceed to Marquette to begin the work of constructing and settling this new church. This was a very arduous journey, via dog sleigh, traveling through the winter snow and ice and finally arriving in February, 1857. In the Spring, Father Duroc oversaw the beginning of construction of a two-story frame building on the corner of Rock and Fourth Street, behind the present day Cathedral. The upper part of that building he occupied himself and celebrated Mass in the lower section.

The second pastor, Father Thiele, arrived in July of 1864 and began the construction of a fairly large church, as he knew the Diocesan See would be transferred from Sault Ste. Marie to Marquette. This church, which would become the Cathedral, was a frame structure of Gothic character based on a stone foundation. Bishop Baraga laid the first cornerstone in his Diocese to this church and dedicated it as the Cathedral in 1866 to Saint Peter, the Apostle.

The first Cathedral was a relatively pretentious building comparing favorable at the time with any church building in the State of Michigan. The cost of construction was $12,000.00 and considerable savings was made by eliminating the sheeting under the siding, therefore, it was almost impossible to heat the church during the winter months. In zero weather the wood furnace had to be fired for three days, night and day, to temper the atmosphere even to a tolerable degree.

There was no turnover in the Pastorate of the Cathedral until Father Edward Jacker became pastor in 1866. Father Jacker was a most intimate friend of Bishop Baraga and helped nurse him through his last illness until his death on January 19, 1868. At this time, Father Jacker became the Diocesan Administrator and appointed Father Edmond Walsh pastor of the Cathedral. Father Jacker remained administrator until Bishop Mrak took up residence in Marquette in February 1869.

In 1870, Father Frederick Eis was ordained by Bishop Mrak and appointed pastor of the Cathedral.

In 1873, a Bishop's residence was built in the rear of the Cathedral from Propagation of the Faith funds. In 1878, Bishop Mrak resigned and Father Jacker again became administrator of the Diocese whereupon he appointed Father John G.Kenny as pastor.

On September 14, 1879 the Rt. Rev. John Vertin was consecrated as the third Bishop of the Sault Ste. Marie and Marquette Diocese at St. Paul's Church in Negaunee. After Bishop Vertin's consecration, Father John C. Kenny, being persona non grata to the new Bishop, was preemptorily removed as pastor of the Cathedral. As an act of vengeance for Father Kenny's removal the Cathedral was set on fire, presumably by some of the parishioners, on October 2, 1879. Bishop Vertin, returning from Negaunee, was greeted by the glare of his burning Cathedral. After the fire the congregation held Mass in the French Church (St. John's) until a new Cathedral was constructed. Bishop Vertin also reinstated Father Kenny as the pastor of the now conflagrated Cathedral at this time. The building committee for the new Cathedral was comprised of Jacob Frei, Balthazar Neidhart,

Henry Erbelding and John Thoney. The cornerstone for the new Cathedral was laid on June 19, 1881, and thereafter, Bishop Vertin acted as pastor.

During the time of the construction, the parishioners of St. Peter's continued to use the French Church. This arrangement **soon** proved to be inadequate to cope with the needs of the two congregations and since the Cathedral was far from being completed, arrangements were made to finish the basement and use it as a church· This was done and the first Mass to be celebrated in the "new" Cathedral was Pontificated by Bishop Vertin on Christmas Eve at Midnight in 1883. The basement continued to be used by the parishioners until July 27, 1890 when the Cathedral was consecrated.

The main altar was a gift of the Bishop's father, Mr. Joseph Vertin of Hancock. The Saint Joseph side altar was a gift from Mr. Joseph Bosch of Lake Linden in memory of his wife, Mary Vertin. The Saint Mary side altar was also donated.

Father J. Langan became the first pastor of the "new"Cathedral in 1890. During his pastorate, a new rectory was built next to the Cathedral at a cost of $4,000.00

In 1899, Father Joseph G. Pinten became pastor and served until 1916. Father Pinten eventually was designated Bishop of Superior, Wisconsin and was consecrated on May 3, 1922 in St. Peter Cathedral. Father Henry A. Buchholtz was appointed pastor in 1916 and held this position until his death in 1945.

Bishop Frederick Eis, who had followed Bishop Vertin as Diocese Head, died on May 5, 1926 and was succeeded by Bishop Paul Joseph Nussbaum. In 1922, a new rectory was constructed at the West side of the Cathedral under the direction of Father Buccholtz for a total cost of $25,000.00. This is the present rectory in use today. On May 16, 1929, Father Buccholtz was elevated to the position of Monsignor and further raised to the rank of Prothonatary Apostolic on July 7, 1934.

In 1930 a tunnel was constructed between the Cathedral and the rectory. As was the custom In many churches prior to this time, the deceased parishioners were often buried next to their church. As the tunnel was being dug underground, the appearance of coffins through the roof of the tunnel occurred on a number of occasions. So, as not to raise the parishioners possible disgust, an undertaker was called in during the evening hours and these coffins were transferred, undetected to the cemetery on the outskirts of town.

Bishop Nussbaum died on June 24, 1935 and Monsignor Buchholtz became Administrator of the Diocese. A second fire struck the Cathedral on Sunday morning, November 3, 1935 at 4:04 A.M. The safety of the Blessed Sacrament was the first concern and Monsignor Buchholtz, with the aid of a fireman, succeeded in getting the tabernacle key from the sacristy. Father Francis Scheringer and Rock Beauchamp, the Cathedral's custodian, were then masked and tied together by a rope, and fought through the smoke and reached the main altar to bring out the Blessed Sacrament. As they reached the safety of the outside door, flames leapt out of the eaves and shortly thereafter, the roof and floor collapsed.

The next morning, Mass was celebrated in the auditorium of Bishop Baraga High School. The auditorium of the high school was used for many months until the basement of the new Cathedral was completed and ready for use for the celebration of Mass.

On January 29, 1936 Bishop Joseph Casimir Plagens was assigned to head the Diocese and was consecrated at the French Church due to the destruction of the Cathedral. During this year, Monsignor Buchholtz was named Vicar General of the Diocese.

The actual building of the new Cathedral began in February of 1936 with the following additions: 1)   it was larger in every way; 2)   the steeples were higher and adorned with colorful blue and red domes with raised crosses covered with gold leaf;. 3)   the nave of the Church was extended; 4)   a Bishop's Chapel was added; 5)   marble altars; 6)   a large painting above the main altar portraying Christ giving to Peter the authority to rule His Church;   7) in the sanctuary, intricate grill work and furnishings of solid oak; 8)   a Bishop's throne of marble and adorned with the coat of arms of Bishop Plagens; 9)   the body of the Church supported by mammoth Romanesque columns;   10) stained glass windows portraying the mysteries of our Lord's life; 11) Stations of the Cross of intricate mosaic and framed in white marble;   12)   statues of varied colored marble;   13)   a Wurlitzer organ and sound system;   14)   the basement redesigned as a modern hall complete with kitchen, storage and utility rooms to provide the parish with facilities for banquets and other activities with a capacity of 600 people.

The building committee of this new Cathedral was comprised of: Anthony Pechaeur (Chairman), Fred Donckers, E. Derhatl, and Harry Kelly. The total cost of the new Cathedral was in excess of $550,000.00 and the money was obtained from donations, fire insurance, $100,000.00 from other parishes of the Diocese and the hard and untiring work of the Cathedral's parishioners.

Services were offered in the new Cathedral proper on September 29, 1937 and the building was completed in September 1938. Formal dedication took place in the Summer of 1939. In December 1940, Bishop Plagens was transferred to the Diocese of Grand Rapids, Michigan and on March 20, 1941 Bishop Francis Manger was installed at the Cathedral. Monsignor Buchholtz died on February 13, 1945 after being pastor of the Cathedral for 29 years, longer than any other priest. Monsignor Buchholtz was so loved and respected by the people of Marquette that on the day of his funeral the businesses in the community closed and the Cathedral could not accommodate the huge crowd of mourners. Father Emil Beyer, who was the assistant at the Cathedral, gave the eulogy. Monsignor John Holland succeeded Monsignor Buchholtz as pastor in March of 1945.

In 1947, the Cathedral was completely redecorated at a cost of $25,000.00 and at this time the mural depicting Christ's presentation of the keys to St. Peter was placed in the niche above the High Altar.

On June 13, 1947 Bishop Francis Magner died and in September 1947, Bishop Thomas Noa was installed as head of the Diocesan See. Monsignor Holland resigned in October 1948 and was succeeded by Father Glen Sanford. Father Sanford was replaced in July 1950 by Father Nolan B. McKevitt who remained pastor of St. Peter's for 25 years during which time he was elevated to Monsignor.

In the 1960's alterations were undertaken to update the recent changes in liturgical worship brought about by the Vatican II Council. The High Altar was no longer used, preference being for the placement of the altar facing the congregation. Therefore, the steps of the sanctuary were extended via the use of a platform, a portable altar placed there, and the use of the Communion railing was discarded.

Bishop Charles Salatka was installed as head of the Diocese on March 25, 1968 and served until his transfer to Oklahoma City in the Fall of 1977. Monsignor McKevitt was replaced in 1975, during Bishop Salatka's period of leadership by Father Louis Cappo who is the present Rector of St. Peter's Cathedral. The present head of the Diocese is Bishop Mark Schmitt who was consecrated and installed on May 8, 1978.

Plans for the redecoration of the Cathedral were begun in 1980 under the combined leadership of Bishop Schmitt and Father Cappo and the work was to be initiated on January 5, 1981. The motivating factors for this new phase of redecoration were two-fold: 1) to enhance the already beautiful Cathedral by instituting a generalized face-lift to include painting and the adaptation of better lighting and 2) to update the Cathedral, as regards to the new liturgical worship format, by bringing the altar closer to the congregation and reserving the Blessed Sacrament in the Bishop's Chapel instead of at the main Altar. The Bishop's Chapel was thus to be renamed, the Chapel of the Blessed Sacrament. The total cost of these changes were an estimated $300,000.00 which was to be shared by the parishioners of St. Peter's, the Diocese of Marquette, and the other parishes in the Diocese on an equal basis.

See Bibliography for reference
information

No significant changes took place at St. Peter Cathedral until 1991 when a new roof was installed. The tile roof was replaced with a new metal roof. The new roof prevented the snow from building up since the snow easily slid off the roof. The work was done by Menze Construction of Marquette, Michigan.

The Diocese of Marquette installed Bishop James H. Garland as the 11th bishop of Marquette on November 11, 1992 at the Cathedral. Prior to his appointment as bishop, he served as an auxiliary bishop in the Archdiocese of Cincinnati. He remained bishop until his retirement on December 13, 2005. As Bishop Emeritus, Bishop Garland continues to reside in Marquette and is frequently present at diocesan events.

In 1992, Perpetual Adoration of the Blessed Sacrament began. Adorers were present in the Blessed Sacrament Chapel for 24 hours a day, 7 days a week, and 365 days a year except when Mass was being celebrated in the main church. It continued until the COVID-19 pandemic in 2020. Today there is an exposition tabernacle which allows the faithful to go and pray before the Blessed Sacrament at any time.

The Cathedral's stained-glass windows are one of many of the features that contribute to the beauty of the worship space. In 1996, Deacon Scott Jamieson submitted the information necessary to register the windows with the Michigan Stained-Glass Census. At this time, care was taken to ensure their integrity from the harsh weather of the Upper Peninsula. The Saint Peter window in the stairwell connecting the gathering space with the rectory and basement came from the old French Church, St. John the Baptist, which had been torn down in the early 1980s. It was installed in 2003 and is therefore not included in the registry.

In 1999, under the direction of Msgr. Louis C. Cappo, the next major renovation was completed. One of the projects that was undertaken was an update to the rectory. It included the addition of a gathering space with a meeting room known as "The Bishop's Room", and an elevator. The elevator was necessary to meet the existing federal regulations mandated by the American Disabilities Act. It provides for access to the additional meeting rooms that were added in the basement during this renovation. These include a Media Room, a small library, and three classrooms. The dedication of these new spaces took place on October 10, 1999. The gathering space was dedicated to Msgr. Cappo and the bronze wall plaque was blessed by Deacon Scott Jamieson. The elevator named in honor of Msgr. Nolan McKevitt also contains a bronze plaque to whom it is dedicated. This renovation was funded entirely by donations of the faithful.

In 2005, parishioner Mark Canale spearheaded the effort to light the towers of the Cathedral. The lighting was paid for through donations from parishioners at the cost of $18,000. The funds for this project were raised giving evidence of the parishioner's love of their Church. The towers were lit for the first time on Christmas Eve of 2005. These lights are a beacon of welcome to the entire community of the city of Marquette. In this same year, the Cathedral was listed on the National Register of Historical Places (no. 12000307).

As mentioned above, Bishop Garland announced his retirement in December of 2005. One of our own diocesan priests, Alexander K. Sample, was ordained as the 12th Bishop of the Diocese of Marquette. His ordination to the episcopacy took place on January 25, 2006. At the time of his ordination, Bishop Sample was the youngest bishop in the United States. The Mass of ordination was celebrated in the presence of a standing-room-only crowd in the Cathedral, which also filled the gathering space and spilled out into the street.

In 2007, the sanctuary was once again renovated. It included the expansion of the predella (altar platform),   the carpeting was removed, and the floor tiled. In order to accommodate this expansion, the seating in the nave of the church was reduced. During the 1981 renovation, the tiles around the statues of the Blessed Mother and St. Joseph, the tile plaques representing the four evangelists that surround the sanctuary, and the tiles under and above the cupola on the back altar had been painted over in the 1981 renovation to "neutralize" their impact. During this renovation, the paint was entirely removed and the pewabic tiles restored to their original beauty. This renovation was completed in 2008.

On March 25, 2008, on the Feast of the Annunciation, EWTN broadcast the Mass. It was an episode of their series, *Cathedrals Across America*. Bishop Sample was the presider at this Mass.

In May of 2012, our first bishop, Frederic Baraga, was declared "Venerable" by Rome, and the Bishop Baraga Chapel was added to the Cathedral. In the fall of 2014, Baraga's body was moved from the Bishops' Crypt to the newly built chapel. Now his body can be publicly accessible for private prayer. The blessing of the chapel took place on October 14 during the annual celebration of Bishop Baraga days. His cause for canonization is currently being examined in Rome, Italy at the Dicastery for the Causes of Saints.

Early in 2013, Bishop Sample was appointed as the new Archbishop of Portland in Oregon. His successor, Bishop John F. Doerfler, a priest from the Diocese of Green Bay, was ordained and installed as the 13th Bishop of the Diocese of Marquette at the cathedral on February 11, 2014.

The COVID-19 pandemic struck in early 2020 and all the churches in the diocese were closed in March. During this time, Sunday Masses were livestreamed from the Cathedral. Bishop John Doerfler was the presider with Msgr. Michael Steber concelebrating and Deacon Thomas Foye assisting. A lector, a musician, and a camera man were the only other authorized individuals in attendance. The parish was reopened in the summer of 2021 and masks were required to be worn by all those in attendance. The seating capacity was reduced with every other pew roped off. The Sign of Peace and Precious Blood were not offered at the Masses due to COVID restrictions.

The latest renovation to the sanctuary began in 2023. A new tabernacle was placed in the main body of the Church on a new altar of repose. The Mensa (meaning "table" in Latin) of the altar of sacrifice (main altar) was enlarged from 5 x 5 feet to 5 x 7 feet. The *cathedra,* or Bishop's Chair, along with the deacon chairs, were moved from the back center of the sanctuary to the St. Joseph side of the sanctuary. The altar server bench was moved to the St. Mary side of the sanctuary. The project was funded by donations from the parishioners and other faithful members of the Diocese. It was completed in the same year. A blessing by Bishop John Doerfler took place at the 10:30am Mass on the First Sunday of Advent of 2023.

REBUILDING OF THE CATHEDRAL - 1936

GENERAL CONSTRUCTION

Bishop Joseph Casimir Plagens, D.D. was installed to head the Diocese of Sault Ste. Marie and Marquette on January 29, 1936. His foremost duty was to be the leading force in the rebuilding of the Cathedral destroyed by fire in the Fall of 1935. He instructed the Cathedral's pastor, Monsignor Henry A. Buchholtz, P.A. to appoint a building committee and start the business of re-building. The appointed building committee consisted of:

> Anthony Pechaeur (Chairman)
> Fred Donckers
> E. Derhatt
> Harry Kelly

[6]

The first order of business was to seek and appoint an architect to draw up the plans and to oversee the rebuilding. The architect selected was:

> Edward A. Schilling, Architect
> 409 Griswold Street
> Detroit, Michigan

The terms of payment to the Architect was to be 8% of the total fee for the general construction and 5% of the total fee for art decoration, marble work, pews, art glass and lighting fixtures. The payments would be made on the first of each month and be computed from the previous months cost. It was estimated that the rebuilding of the Cathedral would be in the area of $250,000.00.

Before any contracts could be awarded, demolition work was necessary to remove the debris from the burned down Cathedral. Archie J. Verville, General Building Construction, Hancock, Michigan was given the job for the demolition work at a fee of $7,500.00.[7] The agreement for the demolition work was as follows:

> THIS AGREEMENT made the sixteenth day of May in the year nineteen hundred and thirty six, by and between ARTHUR J. VERVILLE of Hancock, Michigan, hereinafter called the Contractor and MOST REVEREND JOSEPH CASIMIR PLAGENS, Bishop of

the Diocese of Sault Ste. Marie and Marquette, Michigan,
hereinafter called the Owner.

<u>WITNESSETH</u> that whereas the Owner hereby contracts for
the demolition and salvaging of certain portions of the walls
of the present Cathedral Building as it now stands.

<u>NOW, THEREFORE</u> the Contractor and the Owner, for the
considerations hereinafter named, agree as follows:

<u>Article 1. The Work to be done and the Documents Forming
the Contract.</u>

The Contractor agrees to provide all the labor and materials
and to do all things necessary for the taking down and carefully
salvaging all face stone, as indicated by the drawings bearing
the title: "Stone Salvaging Plan for Marquette Cathedral"
Four sheets of Blue Print Elevations and in Specifications bearing
the same title.

The said Drawings and Specifications and the General
Conditions of the Contract together with this Agreement,
constitute the Contract; the Drawings, Specifications and
General Conditions being as fully a part thereof and hereof as
if hereto attached or herein specified. If anything in the said
General Conditions is inconsistent with this Agreement, the
Agreement shall govern.

The said documents have been prepared by EDWARD A.
SCHILLING, therein and hereinafter called the Architect.

<u>Article 2. The Contractor's Duties and Status.</u>

The Contractor recognizes the relations of trust and
confidence established between him and the Owner by this
Agreement. He covenants with the Owner to furnish his best
skill and judgment and to cooperate with the Architect in
forwarding the interests of the Owner. He agrees to furnish
superintendence and to use every effort to keep upon the work
at all times an adequate supply of workmen and materials
and to secure its execution in the best and soundest way and
in the most expeditious and economical manner consistent with
the interests of the Owner.

<u>Article 3. Fee for Services.</u>

In consideration of the performance of the contract, the
Owner agrees to pay the Contractor, in current funds, as
compensation for his services hereunder an amount not to exceed
SEVEN THOUSAND FIVE HUNDRED DOLLARS called a fixed
fee. In computing the cost of this work, the Contractor shall
be allowed under the terms of this Contract, a profit fee of
10%. He shall also be allowed an overhead fee which shall
not exceed 15% of the actual cost of the work.

Payments for work completed less 15% withheld on or
about the 15th of each month, as certified to by the Architect.

<u>Article 4. Costs to be Reimbursed.</u>

The Owner agrees to reimburse the Contractor in current
funds all costs necessarily incurred for the proper prosecution
of the work and paid directly by the Contractor, such costs

to include the following items, and to be at rates not higher
than the standard paid in the locality of the work except with
prior consent of the Owner.

(a) All labor directly on the Contractor's pay roll.
If overtime shall be necessary or agreed to between Owner and
Contractor, in order to complete the work within a given time,
the basis of time rate for such work shall be agreed upon before
overtime work shall be proceeded with.

(b) Salaries of Contractor's Employees stationed at the
field office, in whatever capacity employed. Employees engaged, at shops or on the road, in expediting the production
or transportation of material, shall be considered as stationed
at the field office and their salaries paid for such part of
their time as is employed on this work.

(c) Any expense required or necessary in procuring of
permits as required by the local authorities.

(d) Any losses sustained by the Contractor not covered
by insurance, provided they have resulted from causes other
than the fault or neglect of the Contractor.

(e) Minor expenses, such as telegrams, telephone service,
expressage, and similar petty cash items.

Article 5. Costs Not to be Reimbursed.

Reimbursement of expenses to the Contractor shall not
include any of the following:

(a) Salary of the Contractor.

(b) Salary of any of the Contractor.

(c) Salary of any person employed in the main branch
office of the Contractor.

(d) Expenses of any kind except those as expressly included in Article 5.

Article 6. Costs to be Paid Direct by the Owner.

In addition to items of cost noted in Article 4 for which
the Owner reimburses the Contractor, the Owner shall pay
all costs as follows:

(a) Materials, supplies and transportation required for
the proper execution of the work, which shall include all temporary structures and their maintenance; all such costs to be
at rates not higher than the standard paid in the locality of
the work except with prior consent of the Owner.

(b) The amounts of all separate contracts.

(c) Premiums on all bonds and insurance policies.

Article 7. Discounts, Rebates, Refunds.

(a) All discounts, rebates and refunds, and all returns
from sale of surplus materials, equipment, etc., shall accrue
to the Owner, and the Contractor shall make provisions so that
they can be secured.

(b) The Contractor will furnish the Owner the cost of
all scaffolding on receiving same and will be charged to the
Owner by the Contractor at its cost price. At the completion

of the work this scaffolding will remain the property of the
Owner.

(c) The contract hereby agrees to leave, at the finish
of his work, such portions of the scaffolding as may be assembled and erected, to remain in place for the use of other
workmen on the job. The balance of all scaffolding not assembled to remain on the premises as property of the Owner for
such disposition as he may elect.

Article 8. Contractor's Financial Responsibility.

Any cost due to the negligence of the Contractor or
anyone directly employed by him, either for the making good
of defective work, disposal of material wrongly supplied, making
good of damage to property, or excess costs for material or
labor, or otherwise, shall be borne by the Contractor, and the
Owner may withhold money due the Contractor to cover any
such cost already paid by him as part of the cost of the work.

This article supersedes the provisions of Articles 12,
13 and 15 of the General Conditions of the Contract so far as
they are inconsistent herewith.

Article 9. Completion of Work.

The Contractor agrees to complete this work on or before
July 11, 1936.

Article 10. Provision for Disposition of Savings.

The Contractor and Owner mutually agree that if the
total of the cost as set forth in Article 3 shall be less than
SEVEN THOUSAND EIGHT HUNDRED DOLLARS ($7,800.00)
then and in that event 50% of such savings shall go to the
Contractor and 50% shall go to the Owner.

Article 11. Accounting, Inspection, Audit.

The Contractor shall check all material and labor entering
into the work and shall keep such full and detailed accounts
as may be necessary to proper financial management under this
Agreement and the system shall be such as is satisfactory to
the Architect and the Owner. The Architect or Owner shall
be afforded access to the work and to all the Contractor's
books, records, correspondence, instructions, drawings, receipts,
vouchers, memorandam, etc. relating to this contract, and the
Contractor shall preserve all such records for a period of one
year after the final payment hereunder.

Article 12. Applications for Payment.

The Contractor shall, between the first and seventh of
each month, deliver to the Architect a statement, sworn to
if required, showing in detail and as completely as possible
all moneys paid out by him on account of the cost of the
work during the previous month for which he is to be reimbursed
under Article 4 hereof, with original pay rolls for labor, checked
and approved by representatives of the Owner of all receipted
bills.

He shall at the same time submit to the Architect a
complete statement of all moneys properly due for materials
or on account of separate contracts, or on account of his fee,

or otherwise, which are to be paid direct by the Owner under
Article 6 hereof.

Article 13. Certificates of Payment.

The Architect shall check the Contractor's statements
of moneys due, called for in Article 12, and shall promptly
issue certificates to the Owner for all such as he approves,
which certificates shall be payable on issuance.

Article 14. Disbursements.

Should the Contractor neglect or refuse to pay, within
five days after it falls due, any bill legitimately incurred by
him hereunder (and for which he is to be reimbursed under
Article 4) the Owner, after giving the Contractor twenty-four
hours written notice of his intention to do, shall have the right
to pay such bill directly, in which event such payment shall
not, for the purpose either of reimbursement or of calculating
the Contractor's fee, be included in the cost of the work.

Article 15. Termination of Contract.

(The provisions of this Article supersede all of Article
37 of the General Conditions of the Contract except the first
sentence).

If the Owner should terminate the contract under the first
sentence of Article 37 of the General Conditions of the Contract, he shall reimburse the Contractor for the balance of all
payments made by him under Article 4, plus a fee computed
upon the cost of the work to date at the rate of percentage
named in Article 3 hereof, or if the Contractor's fee be stated
as a fixed sum, the Owner shall pay the Contractor such an
amount as will increase the payments on account of his fee
to a sum which bears the same ratio to the said fixed sum
as the cost of the work at the time of termination bears to
a reasonable estimated cost of the work completed, and the
Owner shall also pay to the Contractor fair compensation,
either by purchase or rental at the election of the Owner,
for any equipment retained. In case of such termination of
the contract the Owner shall further assume and become liable
for all obligations, commitments and unliquidated claims that the
Contractor may have theretofore, in good faith undertaken or
incurred in connection with said work and the Contractor shall,
as a condition of Receiving the payments mentioned in this
Article, execute and deliver all such papers and take all such
steps, including the legal assignment of his contractural rights,
as the Owner may require for the purpose of fully vesting in
him the rights and benefits of the Contractor under such
obligations or commitments.

The Contractor and the Owner for themselves, their
successors, executors, administrators and assigns hereby agree
to the full performance of the covenants herein contained.

IN WITNESS WHEREOF they have executed this agreement
the day and year first above written.

Archie J. Verville

8

This agreement was to become a very important document because two areas of conflict arose out of the demolition work. One area of conflict was over the contract fee and the other area was over the ownership of the scaffolding. In a letter from Mr. Verville to Mr. Schilling the problem was presented:

> "In checking over the contracts you sent to Monsignor Buchholtz for the wrecking work of the Cathedral, I find that there are several items that are not in accordance with our gentlemen's agreement arrived at on the evening of May 16th at Marquette, viz:
>
> The agreement was that I was to receive 50% reimbursement of the cost of the scaffold materials in addition to the 10% and 15% as well as 50% of the savings if the cost was below $7,500.00. Under Article 7 section (b) of the contract it says, "At the completion of the work this scaffolding will remain the property of the Owner." This is not in accordance with our gentlemen's agreement. In Article 10 of the contract, the amount of the contract reads $7,800.00 when it should be $7,500.00. Will you please correct these items or write new contracts and forward same at once. We signed the contracts before noticing these mistakes."

9

The matter of the contract fee was no problem as Mr. Verville stated he understood the fee to be $7,500.00 not $7,800.00. The matter of the scaf-folding would continue for many months. In June after all the demolition work was done, the following statements were exchanged between Mr. Schilling and Monsignor Buchholtz:

> "Scaffolding clause: In this case, however, if he does not intend to charge in his final statement to you for the scaffold it likewise becomes his property. If, on the other hand, he expects to charge you what he paid for it, it should by all reasoning clear to me, become your property."

10

and

> "I will take up the matter of scaffolding and tools with Mr. Verville. We have paid for all lumber and extra equipment he purchased for this job and hold vouchers and receipted

bills for same. As the contract reads, I do not see how he
can claim part of it, as it distinctly says that all scaffolding
is to revert to the Owner who has paid for it."

[11]

In July, a letter from Mr. Verville stated:

" I hope to be given fair play and without undue delay receive
a settlement in accordance with my original bid for $7,500.00
and take my scaffolding and equipment away from the job or
in accordance with our gentlemen's agreement, leaving the
scaffolding in place for your future use, as per my statement
submitted to you yesterday."

[12]

This matter was given to Anthony Pechauer to handle and many letters were

exchanged between all the parties involved; Mr. Schilling, Mr. Verville,

Monsignor Buchholtz and Mr. Pechauer. These exchanges included references

to the gentlemen's agreement,[13] previously signed contracts,[14] threats of legal

action,[15] and finally a settlement: "I will settle under your terms but under

protest. I will not sue my own church!!"[16] The total paid for the demolition

work was $7,185.74 and the scaffolding remained the property of the Cathedral.[17]

The contract for the labor in connection with the repairing, cutting,

redressing and miscellaneous alterations of the stone work (exterior) of the

Cathedral after the demolition work was finished, was given to: George

Powrie & Sons of Detroit, Michigan.[18] Under the agreement, Mr. Powrie was

to furnish his own tools but the scaffolding, necessary masonry sand, cement

and stone was to be provided by the owner (Cathedral).[19] The rate of pay

to those who did this stone work was:

<u>Supervisor</u>

George Powrie $85.00/week

Peter Hansen $1.25/hour
Jack Marshall
Ernest Watters
Robert Robb
N. Tabor
Harry Powrie

Helpers

Frank Brugman   50¢/hour
W. Vandenbloomer

These men worked eight hours per day and the supervisor at least the same amount of time on the job.[20] The total paid for this phase of the rebuilding was $2,608.75[21] and was finished by the end of June, 1936.

In August, 1936 the following article was released for publication in the Marquette Mining Journal by the Diocesan Office:

"The Most Reverend Joseph C. Plagens, Bishop of the Diocese of Marquette and Building Committee of the Cathedral Parish of St. Peter's of which Monsignor H.A. Buchholtz is pastor, have awarded contracts for the rebuilding of the Cathedral Church.
The General contract has been awarded to: Hutter Bros. of Fond du Lac, Wis..
Heating and Plumbing to: Levine Bros. of this city.
Electrical Work to: V & M Electric Shop of Menominee, Michigan.
The contracts call for the entire completion of these contracts June 1st 1937.
The Contract also provides for occupancy of the basement for temporary church purposes by Christmas. Church services are now held in the Parish hall, pending completion of the building. Under the terms of the contract, the congregation will be able to occupy the finished basement of the building by next Christmas Day.
Because of fire damage, a great deal of the present stone work has been removed and other portions have been replaced and repaired during the time plans and specifications were being completed. The plans provide for the present church to be extended 25 ft. additional in length and to a full width of present church.
A Bishop's Chapel, which was lacking in the old building will be an additional feature of the new building.
This will be on street side toward the rear of the church.

The plans for the new Cathedral will conform to the Romanesque type of building. Many of the most outstanding church buildings of Europe are Romanesque in character, which style antedates the Gothic. The Romanesque is less severe in treatment than other types and lends itself freely to color treatment and decorative motifs which are more or less restricted in the Gothic, Norman types.

The plans for the new building contemplate an interior of dignified proportion with marble columns supporting the Nave ceiling at aisles. The ceiling will be of acoustic tile laid in panels which will combine both the decorative and practical in use, insuring both beauty of treatment and proper acoustics for both Church and Chapel.

The Sanctuary will be finished with marble wainscottings. The Reredos to be of same material as will also the Altars. The Shrines of which there are several will be of Mankato stone and aisles of tile. Major changes are contemplated on the exterior notably on the facade, which will be featured by a large window in keeping with the gable height. The towers will be terminated with a dome feature characteristic of this style of building. This feature of the building has been carefully considered and studied from plaster models designed to accurate scale from the Architects details. The exterior of Chapel will harmonize in design to the Main Church and will be a pleasing addition to exterior and greatly enhance the entire mass of the structure.

The Chapel of which mention is previously made is to be dedicated to the memory of Bishop Baraga, first Bishop of Marquette. In keeping with traditional practice of the Catholic Church, the remains of the bishop are buried in the Cathedral's Crypts. The new crypt has been carefully planned in the basement of the Chapel. When completed, the bodies of the three former bishops now in present crypt will be removed to the new section. The crypt will have a separate entrance from tower leading to Chapel. It is featured by an octagonal vestibule separated from crypt proper by wrought iron gates and finished in brick and marble with floors of inlaid tile.

Monsignor Buchholtz, the pastor, has been delegated by Bishop Plagens to assume full charge of the work for the Parish and will be assisted in this by the Building Committee which is composed of: Anthony Pechauer, Fred Donckers, E. Derhatt and Harry Kelly. They will cooperate with the Bishop and Architect in the selection of all materials and furnishing and the furtherance of all matter pertaining to the proper completion of the building.

Edward A. Schilling of Detroit, who is the Architect for this building has designed many of the outstanding church buildings in Detroit, his home city, as well as others throughout the state."

22

The Hutter Construction Co., 124 Western Avenue, Fond du Lac, Wisconsin
was awarded the general construction contract for $231,000.00. (Table I)[23]
They estimated the bid from the general contract specifications released by
the architect, Mr. Schilling. (Table II)[24] The contract between the Hutter
Construction Company and the Diocese of Marquette can be read in Table X.

The plumbing and heating contract was awarded to Levine Bros., Heating
and Plumbing, 219 W. Washington Street, Marquette, Michigan for $21,915.88.
(Table IX)[25] Immediately there was confusion as to the most reliable type
of coal stoker to be used for heating the Cathedral. Mr. H. J. Runnings,
the mechanical engineer for Levine Bros., recommended the Detroit Stoker
over the Butler Stoker for the following reasons:

1) The Butler Stoker has stationary side plates and is a worm
   type of operation.

2) The Detroit Stoker is a ram type of operation.

3) Worm type stokers are more likely for replacement under
   average usage than the ram type of Detroit.

4) Ash accumulation in the Butler Stoker is through the firing
   door, whereas in the Detroit Stoker is through the ash pit
   and can be raked out.

[26]

Mr. Schilling received letters from the following individuals recommending
the Butler Stokers:

        Isidore Diebold, O.S.B., Pastor
        St. Mary's Church
        Maryville, Mo.

[27]

        T. Werth, Pastor
        St. Bernard's Church
        Thief River Falls, Minn.

[28]

E. J. Lusiere, Pastor
St. Joseph's Church
Rid Lake Falls, Minn.

29

Rev. Henry D. Paneiz
Olivia, Minn.

30

Frank Bruce, Publisher
The Catholic School Journal
Milwaukee, Wis.

31

As can be imagined, the controversy over the type of stoker to be used was intense and frustrating but it was finally decided to install the Detroit Ram-Type Stoker.

The electrical work was awarded to V & M Electric Co. of Menominee, Michigan for $3,447.00.[32] This work was to cover all the wiring and fixtures to be placed in the Cathedral. The larger lighting fixtures were put out for bids to the following companies:

Gezelschap & Sons
Lighting Fixtures, Heating and Ventilating
Milwaukee, Wisconsin

Detroit Mantel and Tile Company
Lighting Fixtures
1431 Farmer Street
Detroit, Michigan

Lightalier Company
Jersey City, New Jersey

The contract for the larger fixtures was awarded to the Detroit Mantel and Tile Company for $6,921.60.[33]

After these contracts were awarded, the general construction was begun with the goal being the completion of the basement for celebration of Midnight Mass on December 24, 1936. In August, 1936, Monsignor Buchholtz wrote to the Hutter Company:

> "The work is progressing nicely, and if the Lord favors us
> with good weather we hope you will be able to get us into
> the basement by Christmas."

34

As with all construction, there are changes from the original specifications which formed the initial contract between the involved parties. (Table X) During the rebuilding of the Cathedral there were such changes. The first change that was encountered was that of the choir loft. Initially it was to be built entirely of wood but, after reviewing the blueprints, it was decided to reinforce the choir loft with steel and concrete, then face it with oak.

> "As per your telegraphic request of today, we contacted
> the Truscon Steel Company relative to changing the choir
> gallery construction from wood to bar joist and placing
> thereon a 2½" concrete slab with sleepers ready to receive
> the finished wood floor originally specified. . . . . extra
> cost of $274.00."

35

There were many questions and subsequent changes regarding the interior stone that was used in the Cathedral. The interior stone was originally to be cream Mankato stone but, due to cost and availability, it was necessary to switch from complete stone on the side walls to partial stone. The wainscoting was maintained in Mankato stone but the remaining side walls were done in cast plaster in such a way as to match this stone.[36]

At this time, the feasibility of having all the columns done in the Mankato stone was also discussed. The initial contract stated that the round columns were to be done in scagliola, which is a mixture of plaster and marble that is polished. Also, these columns are hollow when constructed with scagliola and an increase in weight would result if Mankato stone was substituted. After correspondence between Hutter, Schilling and Buchholtz it was decided to maintain the scagliola columns because:

1) The price would be approximately $8,000.00 more if Mankato stone was used.

[37]

2) There would be an increase of 15,000 lbs. of floor weight which would severly compromise the structural design.

[38]

By now it was also known that there would be a shortage of the natural Marquette snadstone used on the exterior facade to increase the height of the twin towers at the front of the Cathedral and the small tower near the Chapel. Many solutions were discussed as to this shortage but it was finally settled to use a rough finished brown stone on the upper portions of the towers as a substitute for the sandstone. This was an increase of $2,3000.00 over the initial contract agreement.[39] Later, while reviewing the original cost and extra cost, it was determined that there would be a decrease of $1,000.00 on this total as previously figured.[40]

The next problem that arose was whether a better floor material, terrazzo, should be substituted for the originally planned Gibraltar floor at an increased price. Since the Gibraltar floor was nothing more than a cement floor with a $\frac{1}{4}$" top dressing monolithically applied and the terrazzo floor was the same cement floor 2 3/4" thick with a 5/8" terrazzo topping, it was felt the terrazzo floor would withstand more wear and tear over the ensuing years. It would mean an increase of $2,730.00 over the original contract but it would pay for itself in the future. It was decided to use terrazzo on all the areas of the floor including all risers and platforming. It was felt that the floor, when done in a neat form of patterns and colors, would really make a splendid job. This would include all the flooring in the basement as an extra.[41]

Since the question of flooring was being discussed, it was felt that the confessionals should be maintained in wood. This decision was later changed and these floors were done with asphalt tile.[42]

During this period, the wainscoting in the basement had been changed from the original Mankato stone to Bufftone Brictile and this extra Mankato stone was used for the four square columns in the main church.[43]

At this time, an interesting amount of correspondence was going on between Monsignor Buchholtz and Mr. Schilling as regards the questions of doors vs. drapes on the confessionals. It was decided:

> "I think I would prefer a nice heavy drape on the penitents' part of the confessionals. The priests' part to be equipped with a door."

[44]

Also, the feasibility of communicating from the confessionals was discussed. It was decided to install a buzzer system from the sacristy to the house, from the sacristy to the choir, and from the confessionals to the house.[45] Those of us who remember this buzzer system can recall the shattering of our repose during Mass when the system was in action. This was just another one of those "little" extras that had been overlooked with the original specifications.

One area of controversy that was present during the rebuilding of the Cathedral and which would continue to cause many problems, even into the redecorating instituted in early 1981, was that of the ceiling and roof. The roof was constructed of wood planking and reinforced with angle iron supports between the trusses. As early as August, 1936, there were questions over the use of wood planking due to the possibility of increased fire hazzard. It was explained at that time that the roof was of structural steel and only the top and purlins were of wood and plank. The entire ceiling was hung from steel members, no wood being used, and all the finished ceiling on the surface was of plaster or fireproof material. The few lights under the roof were run in metal cables. After reviewing these facts, there would be no savings on the insurance premiums if the roof was gypsum plank so it was decided to maintain the original construction plans and not make any roof or ceiling changes.[46] In 1939 it was found that some of the exterior tiles were falling from the roof. It was found that this problem was caused by the high humidity in the ceiling-roof interspace which caused the planking to become moist then shrink due to the high heat on the roof. This shrinkage sheared the copper nails holding the roofing tiles and they dislodged. To correct this problem, additional angle iron supports were placed to compensate for this shrinkage.[47] [48] Today, the roofing tiles still occasionally fall from the Cathedral roof.

The ceiling displayed varying degrees of discoloration after the rebuilding. Initially, this discoloration was felt to be dirt but as it turned out, it was much more involved and unsolvable. As to the problem of the ceiling tiles and their discoloration, it is related to the type of insulation used in the rebuilding construction. An insulation called "Sprayo-Flake" was installed contrary to the recommendations of Mr. Schilling. Mr. Schilling was informed that some jobs where this type of insulation was used showed discoloration in the ceiling following hot weather.[49] Essentially, "Sprayo-Flake" is composed of paper and a mastic base. Thus, it is subject to run or flow during hot weather and in some cases, leakes through and discolors ceilings. Apparently, it was felt that Marquette didn't experience enough "hot" weather to have this problem of discoloration occur.[50] This problem area of the roof and ceiling was never fully corrected after the rebuilding of the Cathedral. Those of us who have ever looked up at the ceiling remember how discolored it had become over the years.

When the Cathedral was nearing completion there was a problem with the vestibule doors which Mr. Schilling happened to notice. He wrote to Rock Beauchamp, who was the Cathedral's janitor, the following:

> "When we were leaving the Cathedral, we noticed that some of the door holders which are fastened into expansion shields on the outside were loose and screwed out. Is it possible that the kids have fun doing this? If so, we believe that the Sisters should be told to advise the children not to destroy Church property and to leave their fingers off these fastenings. After all, they are very serviceable when they are securingly screwed into place but absolutely of no value if the kids keep monkeying with them."

51

When the original bid was submitted by the Hutter Construction Company, the cost of the construction of the Bishop's Chapel was not included. The Chapel was built at the same time of the general reconstruction and the total cost was $23,332.50 which did not include electrical fixtures, art glass, furniture and decorating.[52] This was considered to be an "extra" to the initial bid.

In the final analysis of costs I refer you to Tables IV, V, VI, VII and VIII at the end of this paper. Among the architect, general contractor, electrical contractor and plumbing & heating contractor the following represent their final billings:

<u>Architect (Mr. Edward A. Schilling)</u>

Contract:	$23,883.89
Extras:	3,556.96
Credits:	−203.78
TOTAL:	$27,237.07

General Contractor (Hutter Construction Co.)

    Contract: $231,000.00
    Approved Extras: 18,888.40
    Unapproved Extras: 11,324.89

        TOTAL: $261,213.29

Electrical Contractor (V & M Electric Co.)

    Contract: $3,447.00
    Approved Extras: 1,609.90

        TOTAL: $5,056.90

Plumbing & Heating Contractor (Levine Bros.)

    Contract: $21,915.88
    Approved Extras: 963.18

        TOTAL: $22,879.06

A letter from Mr. George F. Hutter to Monsignor H. A. Buchholtz reflects

the shared cooperation present during the reconstruction of the Cathedral.

> "In closing, I want to speak for myself and my associates
> that we have never enjoyed a building operation any more
> than to have been privileged to build your new Cathedral.
> The splendid cooperation which we have always had from
> Bishop Plagens, yourself, and all others interested, has made
> what appeared at one time to be a tough job, a most pleasant
> and happy transaction."

53

SPECIFIC CONSTRUCTION

STAINED GLASS

The T. C. Esser Co., of Milwaukee, Wisconsin, submitted proposals for the glass work in the two main church towers, the gallery floor, the baptistry, and the Bishop's Chapel tower. These proposals were accepted for the sum of $1,245.00 and were as follows:

"For the sum of Nine Hundred Sixty Five ($965.00) Dollars, we propose to furnish the following windows in the tower of St. Peter's Cathedral, as per specifications of Architect Edw. A. Schilling:

No. 1: Eight upper tower windows, to be leaded in rectangular design as per submitted pencil sketch. The glass to be used in these windows is according to the architect's specifications, English Double Rolled Glass, in four different tints, subject to the architect's selection. These windows are to be leaded entirely in $\frac{1}{2}$" lead, with the necessary steel enforcing bars.

No 2: Four gallery floor tower windows, to be leaded in geometric design, as shown in pencil sketches submitted. The background of these windows is to be four tints of English Double Rolled Glass, the border in richer tones; colors to be subject to the selection of the architect. These windows are to be leaded principally in $\frac{1}{2}$" lead, with inter-lacing parts of the windows in 3/8" lead. These windows are to be fitted with the necessary steel enforcement bars.

No. 3: Two baptistry and one nartex window executed as shown in submitted color sketch; subject to modifications by the architect. These three windows are to be made of Imported German and English Antique Glass exclusively, to be painted and fired, and the tracery on the background of tints to be enriched with a soft gold effect through applied silver. Each of these windows to contain a symbol, subject to selection of Monsignor H. A. Buchholtz, P.A..

These windows are to be set in steel sash, embedded in putty, and installed with the necessary strengthening bars to give sufficient protection against wind pressure.

This proposal includes also the removal of the present tower windows.

54

and,

"I wish to confirm our conversation regarding the windows
for the stairway and tower in the Bishop's Chapel, which
we propose to install for the sum of Two Hundred Eighty
($280.00) Dollars, and which price you kindly accepted."

55

The total sum, after extras for additional glass and glazing, which included

replacement due to damage and changes in the original proposal came to

$1,885.39.

The specifications and blueprints for the remainder, also the majority,

of the stained glass in the main Church and the Bishop's Chapel was forwarded

to the following firms on April 20, 1937.

    T. C. Esser - Milwaukee, Wisconsin
    Rambusch Decorating Co. - New York, New York
    Wilber H. Burnham - Boston, Massachusetts
    Willette Art Glass Co. - Philadelphia, Pennsylvania
    Detroit Stained Glass Co. - Detroit, Michigan
    Pittsburgh Stained Glass Co. - Pittsburgh, Pennsylvania
    Henry Schmidt - Willmette, Illinois
    Conrad Schmidt - Milwaukee, Wisconsin
    Munich Art Glass Co. - New York, New York

56

The specifications were drawn up by Edward A. Schilling, Architect of Detroit,

Michigan as follows:

<u>SCOPE OF WORK:</u>

This specification contemplates the furnishing and
installation complete for twenty-five (25) stained glass
windows as selected by the Bishop, Pastor and Architect
from designs received.

In submitting estimates, consideration must be given
to the windows being installed as funds permit. All windows, however, will be selected from the designs of one
firm.

<u>RECEIVING OF BIDS:</u>

Bids will close May 28, 12 o'clock Noon.

INTERIOR WALL TREATMENT

GENERAL COLOR SCHEME OF INTERIOR:

For benefit of bidders and the consideration of interior wall color in relation to glass colors it is to be noted that the finished interior of Nave is of a light buff tone.

SKETCHES & DESIGNS:

Size of drawing at option of designer. All drawing to have one window presented in color. If accompanying drawings are submitted for other windows, they may be in pencil or other medium.

Each bidder must submit exact glass samples to be used in accordance with the terms of their bid.

In the absence of sketches or drawings, a bidder must submit an assembled glass sample not less than 24" x 60" in size indicating general character of leading, coloring border and portion of type of design, contemplated by his estimate.

The submission of an assembled glass design in addition to sketches is optional with other bidders but not required.

All windows are to be Romanesque in type and developed in a rugged rather than a finished character. Extremes of modern or too early types in depicting the features of subjects is to be avoided.

COMPOSITION OF DESIGN

TRANSEPT WINDOWS:

The two transept windows comprise a group of three windows each (See blueprint). The center one of each group to be featured with a figure subject. One, "Christ the King", the other Mary, "Queen of Heaven". (Suggested by Bishop). One of these preferred for submitted design.

Side windows comprising each group at discretion of designer subject to selection of actual design by Bishop or Pastor.

Borders of rich dark tones in contrast to field or in harmony with main motif.

CHOIR WINDOWS:

Three in group. (See blueprint). Subject – of Main Center Window – St. Cecelia – David and choir of Angels or similar subject as approved. Side windows at option of designer. Subject to future approval of design. Borders as heretofore specified.

NAVE WINDOWS:

Ten in all. (See blueprints). Figure subjects of Cannonized

Bishops. Personages as hereafter designated. In designing
the three inside well windows of Chapel and one in Nave
over entrance to Chapel consideration should be given to these
three windows being artificially reflector-lighted during day-
time services.

<u>GLASS:</u>

All glass to be antique. If a percentage of Norman
Slabs are contemplated by the Bidder, it is to be mentioned
in Bid. All painted portions to be kiln fired. Leading to
be antique in character. Width of leads as required for the
appropriateness of design. All leads are to be well soddered.
Glass cement to be of standard quality composed of white
lead putty, litharge and whiting. Puttying to be on both sides
of glass to make thoroughly weathertight.
Present division bars are of galvanized steel. All to be
reinforced as required to make a thoroughly secure installation
in accordance with best practice. All glass to be thoroughly
bedded and to be left clean and in good condition at completion
of the work.
Should any leakage occur, the contractor shall upon notification, make same weathertight.

57

The contract was awarded to the Detroit Stained Glass Works, 4831-
4833 Fort Street West, Detroit, Michigan for the sum of $20,092.00. Their
proposal was as follows:

"We propose to furnish the Stained Glass Windows for St. Peter's
Roman Catholic Cathedral, Marquette, Michigan, as per our de-
signs and as specified and under the supervision of Mr. Schilling,
Architect and equal to sample medallion which we have submitted.

Chapel Windows. (6)
To contain single figures of Bishops and with medallion in base
of windows.

Nave Aisle Windows. (10)
To contain three medallions each. West Elevation to have the
fifteen mysteries of the rosary and the East Elevation, scenes
from the life of Christ.

Large Center Transept Windows. (2)
One to contain Mother, Queen of Heaven and Adoring Angels
and six apostles and the second window to contain Christ,
the King and Adoring Angels and six Apostles.

Small Side Transept Windows. (4)
To contain the four Evangelists and Symbol Medallion in top
of each window and Medallion in base of each window.

Choir Window. (3)
To contain the figures of the musical saints: St. Cecilia,
St. Ambrose, St. David and St. Gregory and five adoring
Angels.

Windows to be installed as directed and our price includes
complete installation in church.

6 Chapel Windows	$ 267.00	each	$ 1,602.00
10 Aisle Windows	1,050.00	each	10,500.00
2 Large Transept Windows	1,440.00	each	2,880.00
4 Small Transept Windows	630.00	each	2,520.00
1 Center Choir Window	1,110.00	each	1,110.00
2 Side Choir Windows	740.00	each	1,480.00

$20,092.00   "

58

The contract was accepted and signed on July 28, 1937.

After the windows were fabricated and placed in the Cathedral the

following newspaper article was published by the Marquette Mining Journal

on February 19, 1938:

New Stained Glass Windows Are Installed In Cathedral

Stained glass windows for the east and west transepts
in the new St. Peter's Cathedral have been installed. They
were designed and made by the Detroit Stained Glass works
under the direction of Edward A. Schilling, of Detroit, the
Cathedral architect.

The east, or Christ the King window, contains in the
center uppermost part Christ the King surrounded with
Angels and Cherubs encircled with symbols of Christ, the
Alpha and Omega, Chi Rho, X.P. and I.H.C. below which
are the six apostles, St. James Minor, St. Peter, St. John,
St. Andrew, St. Bartholemew and St. Phillip, each known by
their symbol which is interwoven in the glass above each
figure. Below these figures are symbols of Christ, the Chalice,
Agnus Dei and the Font.

In the smaller side transept opening, two of the evangelists,
St. Matthew and St. Mark, are placed with their symbols above
them. And below these full-sized figures are scenes representing
the Holy Sacraments of baptism and confirmation.

At the base of these openings are placed the "Lamp and Bible" and the "Crown of Thorns" - symbols of Christ.

This group of windows is in memory of the Werner family and is the gift of Fred and Jacob Werner.

The west Mother Queen of Heaven window contains in the center uppermost part Mary the Queen, surrounded with Angels and Cherubs encircled with symbols of Mary, Gate of Heaven, star and crescent Flur dy Lys and the Pierced Heart, below which are the other six apostles, St. Thomas, St. Paul, St. James Major, St. Jude, St. Simon and St. Matthias, also distinguished by their symbols which have been placed above them. Below these figures symbols of Mary, Fountain, Ave Maria and the Anchor appear.

In the outer west transept panels the figures of the other two evangelists, St. Luke and St. John have been placed together with their symbols above them and scenes representing the Sacraments of matrimony and extreme unction. Below them and in the bases of these windows have been placed Mary's symbols of the lilies and the mystical rose.

This group of windows is in memory of the Neidhardt family and is the gift of Miss Lena Neidhardt.

The choir window was installed two months ago. This is a musical window and contains figures of St. Cecilia, St. Ambrose, St. Gregory and King David, with the figures surrounded by adoring angels with musical instruments - - trumpet, cymbals, drum and triangle. The Dove of the Holy Ghost is placed in the top of the center lancet and symbols of Christ in the bottom of the window.

This window is in memory of Mr. and Mrs. Martin Vierling, Sr., and is the gift of Mr. and Mrs. A. L. Heutter.

59

The pew specifications were drawn up by Edward A. Schilling, Architect, of Detroit, Michigan. Bids were to be received by 6 P.M., September 25, 1936. The specifications were as follows:

"The seats are to be built in accordance with the layout, Sheet No. 128, providing for all back and front screens which are to be in accordance with details.

The back and seats are to be constructed of 5-ply material with center core 9/36" in thickness and intermediate sections between core and face 1/8" with grain at right angle to adjoining layers. The backs and seats are to be in profile as indicated by the Sectional Drawings.

The top rail of seat back is to be finished with a molded rail as detailed and to extend full length of each back and to be housed into pew ends.

Each pew is to have a center support of standard type or as approved. The front edge of each seat is to be finished with a molded edge as indicated by the design. Water proof bottom of each pew seat with an approved paint.

Each seat is to be supplied with statuary bronze numbers as selected and these are to be applied to the pews by this contractor where so instructed by the Pastor or Architect.

BOOK RACKS:

Each pew is to be supplied with 2-30" book racks. The center of each to be placed about 4 ft. from end of pew back.

PEW ENDS:

The Pew ends are designed for two (2) distinct types, numbered Design 1 and Design 2.

Bids are to be submitted on both types and in submitting figure indicated as Design 1 and Design 2. Pew ends are to be $2\frac{1}{4}$" in thickness. Design 2 to be provided with seat housing bracket as indicated.

CARVING:

Where indicated on Design 1, provide a carved panel on each seat which may be machine roughed and hand carved finish.

In machining, care is to be taken not to destroy under-cutting where this occurs. This carved unit must be in accordance with a model which is to be approved by the Architect before any cutting is done. One panel at each seat end.

<u>SEAT BRACKETS:</u>

Provide seat brackets at pew ends where necessary to insure rigid construction.

<u>MATERIAL:</u>

All seats are to be constructed of straight grained Appalachian White Oak.

All facing material shall be of resawed lumber and not less than 1/8" in thickness and all edge glued.

Face material to be cut from the same flitch so as to insure uniformity of grain.

<u>FINISH OF SEATS:</u>

(1) Seats are to be stained with a good wood stain, color as selected by Architect (The Seating Company to submit color samples for matching or selection).

(2) Apply one (1) coat of Lacquer or Spar Varnish of standard quality.

(3) Sandpaper lightly to remove all uneveness.

(4) One (1) coat of Spar Varnish.

(5) Rub to semi-dull finish with pumice stone and oil.

When seats are set, any seat out of proper alignment or otherwise untrue in form or unacceptable will be rejected and must be immediately corrected to the satisfaction of the Architect.

Provide oak kneeling benches for each pew as indicated by the drawings. Each bench to have hardware of approved type to permit bench to be raised back if necessary. Each kneeler to have bracketed supports to insure rigidity.

All bids are to be submitted as follows:
A - Design 1 - Standard finish
B - Design 1 - finish as specified
C - Design 2 - Standard finish
D - Design 2 - finish as specified
E - Design 1 - Omitting carved panel

60

The following companies presented bids for the placement of the pews:

The Manitowoc Church Furniture Co.
Waukesha, Wisconsin

The American Seating Company
Ninth and Broadway
Grand Rapids, Michigan

The American Seating Company of Grand Rapids, Michigan was awarded the contract for a fee of $6,483.00[61] The final fee, after the addition of extras, was $6,739.75. The pew end was No. 9617 which was different from that of the specifications. This pew end appeared as below:

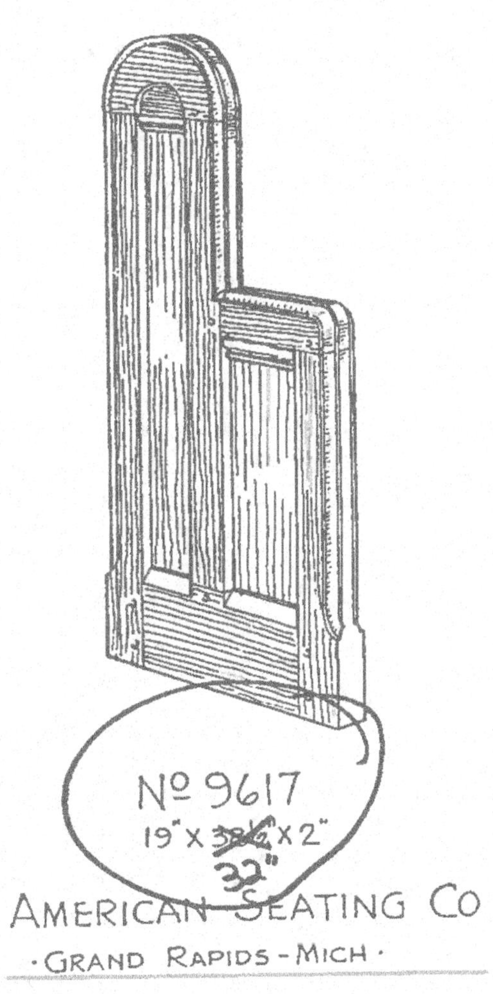

62

After the pews were placed, two letters were received, one by Monsignor Buchholtz and one by the American Seating Company, as regards to the comfort of the kneelers. The letter received by Monsignor Buchholtz contained the following:

> "May I mention the matter of kneelers with which you are as familiar as myself. I was told only yesterday that the church was fine except that the kneeling benches were very badly placed and uncomfortable. I also got this same criticism from the chief of your local Fire Department, also from two of the Hotel Northern employees who are members of the church. In view of this, I feel it is apparently one outstanding objection that should, if possible, be eliminated. The benches which were corrected towards the front end are O.K. and I believe the sooner some action is taken to change the balance it will be a correction that will be generally appreciated by your entire congregation."
>
> 63

The letter received by the American Seating company included:

> "Gentlemen:
>
> Your Company was privileged to furnish the Seating for the above project and we happen to be the General Contractors but, as you will recall, the Seating was purchased under a separate contract and, no doubt, your attention has been called to the fact that the Seating as it is now set is most uncomfortable, because it is utterly impossible for anyone to stand in an erect position due to the fact that the kneelers do not permit standing erect, and the only solution to the problem, as we see it, would be to move the kneelers forward.
>
> You may be surprised to have a letter from us, but you will recall that your Company has been associated on Building Projects which we have erected, throughout the United States, a great many times, and this is what we are encountering. When we meet people and they comment on St. Peter's Cathedral at Marquette, Michigan, they usually follow it up by saying, 'Boy! you certainly made a mess of the Pews.' You can appreciate how hard it is for us to tell the people we had nothing to do with either the manufacture or the setting of these Pews. While it might be true that you followed drawings and details, nevertheless, I do recall only this last summer when one of your Representatives stressed the point that your Company were pioneers in arranging for the proper posture so as to afford comfort.

We do not believe that your Company can afford to have the
condition that now exists at Marquette, Michigan, continue
without correcting it and - after all, a few good mechanics
would move those kneelers in a very short time - about all
they need is authority from your Company and, personally,
we do not believe that you should delay putting these Pews
in a comfortable position any longer."

64

The matter of the kneelers was corrected as best as feasibly possible but

those of us who had the opportunity to use the old pews before the 1981

rennovation have fond memories of their lack of comfort.

<u>MARBLE ART</u>

The original plans for the construction of three altars, shrines and stations of the cross were that these pieces would be made of carved white oak and finished in a bronze stain effect. The specifications for this wood work were drawn up and to be executed by the International Statuary and Altar Co., 128-130 E. North Avenue, Milwaukee, Wisconsin. This company was the American representative for the world famous Moroder studies in Tyral since 1866. The proposal for these altars and shrines and the esti- mated fees were as follows:

Bishop's Chapel Altar	$2,064.00
Shrine of the Little Flower	950.00
St. Joseph's Altar	586.00
Blessed Virgin Altar	586.00
Shrine of St. Anne	800.00
Shrine of Our Lady of Perpetual Help	850.00
Shrine of the Sacred Heart	550.00
Stations of the Cross	1,820.00
TOTAL:	$8,206.00

65

This company also presented a proposal for the marble work to be ex- ectued at the Cathedral. This marble work included the main altar, tabernacle, communion railing, mosaics, pewabic tile work, statues and emblems of the evangelists. In a follow-up letter from the company's representative, A.J. Moroder, he promised a $500.00 donation if they received the bid. The reason for this was: "I was two full years sick, Poisened Gums, and Doctor gave the hope up, telling my wife and children that this is a hopeless case. ..... and about the Month of March, the sickness became null, and I can work better than ever, So I decidet [sic] to give, in case I am honored with the Order for the Diocese of Marquette Cathedral."[66]

After considering the differences between marble and wood construction, it was decided that all of the previous work that was to be done in white oak was to be done in marble. This work was given to the International Statuary and Altar Co. for the sum of $10,032.00 which included the above mentioned $500.00 donation.[67]

The work was progressing at a satisfactory pace when Mr. Schilling was informed that Mr. A. J. Moroder was compelled to withdraw from all past and further negotiations concerning the work for the Marquette, Michigan Cathedral because he was suffering a complete nervous breakdown.[68]

At this time, the Giuseppe Tommasi Studies, Ecclesiastical Art Marble Specialists, Pietiasanta, Carrara (Italy), New York, and Chicago, 840 N. Michigan Avenue, Chicago, Illinois were preparing the marble–mosaic Stations of the Cross.[69] (A blueprint of one station can be found at the end of this section of the paper). It was decided to approach them and have them bid for the finishing of the discontinued marble work. They made the following proposal which was accepted:

Altars and railing	$13,760.00
Shrines and Stations	12,000.00
Bishop's Throne and Sedillia	5,000.00
TOTAL:	$30,760.00

[70]

The contract contained the following work description for the Shrines and Statues for the Cathedral:

SCOPE OF WORK

(A) – SHRINE MOTHER OF PERPETUAL HELP
Includes complete design as indicated painting furnished by Owner. Statues of trani marble.

(B)   -   <u>SHRINE OF THE LITTLE FLOWER</u>
          Includes base and statue of varigated marbles and
          coat of arms as approved to replace original emblem
          indicated.

(C)   -   <u>SHRINE OF SAINT ANNE</u>
          Includes base and statues. Statues to be built of
          varigated marbles.

(D)   -   <u>SHRINE OF SACRED HEART</u>
          Including base and statues built of varigated marbles.

(E)   -   <u>STATUES OF ST. JOSEPH & MARY ALSO SIDE ALTARS</u>
          To be of varigated marbles. Figures of two angels,
          painting main dome to be of same varigated marble.

(F)   -   The two following items omitted from and relating
          to altar contract under date of Feb. 15, 1938 are
          to be included and executed as part of this contract:

          (1)   The Interior Dome of Main Altar to
                be of venetian colored mosaic subject
                of decoration to be as approved by the
                Bishop.

          (2)   The face of the base of Little Flower
                Shrine is to have coat of arms to
                replace that now indicated on blue-
                prints. (Material as approved).

                                                    71

During the course of work on the marble a number of changes occurred

which are noted as follows:

"You will note that the change requested on the Little Flower
Shrine has been made and that a coat of arms of the Carmelite
Order has replaced the three flowers. You also will note, that
the Crucifix held by the Little Flower has been raised some-
what and that roses have been placed into her arms."

                                                    72

"The Tabernacles for the Shrines of St. Anne and the Sacred
Heart have been eliminated and in their place an ornamental
panel has been designed, which will provide ample space for
a Crucifix."

                                                    73

"On the Stations of the Cross, the number has been put below
the Mosaic as requested."

                                                    74

"Our Lord in priestly vestments and two children at His feet –
for the center Mosaic of the Blessed Sacrament Chapel."

75

As the marbles and mosaics that were used in the fabrication of the
altars, shrines, statues, and stations of the cross were being shipped from
Italy, a letter declaring these items as true and permanent works of art, was
necessary to avoid customs duty. The following instructions from the Tommasi
Studios was sent with the specifics as regards this customs approval:

Re: St. Peter's Cathedral, Marquette, Mich.

LIST OF LETTERS OF ACCEPTANCE AND PRESENTATION
ISSUED IN DUPLICATE FOR THE ITEMS AS FOLLOWS:

Marble High Altar.
Marble Side Altar including the Statue of the Blessed Virgin.
Marble Side Altar including the Statue of St. Joseph.
Marble Altar of the Blessed Sacrament including six Angel
   statues and the mosaic panel of Christ-Priest.
Marble Altar Railing including bronze gates.
Marble Shrine of Little Flower including statue.
Marble Shrine of Our Lady of Perpetual Help.
Marble Shrine of Sacred Heart including statues.
Marble Shrine of St. Anne including statues.
Fourteen Stations of theCross in mosaic with marble frame.

NOTE: All letters of Acceptance, original and duplicate,
          must be signed by the Right Rev. Msgr. Henry A.
          Buchholtz, P.S., V.G., Rector.

Letters of Presentation, original and duplicate, must be signed
by the donors of the above items. Each donor must sign only
the letters in which is written the item he donated. If there
is a donor which donated two or more items, for example the
two Side Altars, he must sign both letters in which these altars
are mentioned. Supposed that one Side Altar or Shrine is
donated by one donor and the statue on same by another,
the letter (original and duplicate) must be signed by both donors.

With regard to the Stations of the Cross, if each one is donated
by a different donor, the letter (original and duplicate) must
be signed by all 14 donors or by less if two, three or more
stations are donated by one donor.

If some of the items, supposed the Stations of the Cross or
the High Altar etc., is donated by a Society, for example

the Holy Name Society, the St. Patrick Society, the Sanctuary
Society or by a Committee etc., the letters, always original
and duplicate, can be signed by the President of the Society
or Committee.

All the signed letters of Acceptance and Presentation, in duplicate,
must be sent to the Giuseppe Tommasi Studios, 590 West 172nd
Street, New York, N.Y., on or before June 4th, 1938."

76

All of the afore mentioned works of art were delivered in excellent condition

and can be seen in the Cathedral.

As mentioned earlier in this section of the paper, the original work

was to be done in wood. Before the decision was made to change to marble,

the International Statuary and Altar Co. was commissioned to fabricate and

deliver a Christmas crib with the figures. The panorama crib was 8 feet

wide by 8 feet long by 4 feet high and the figures were 16 inces high.[77]

This is the crib and figures that are used presently during the Nativity

season at the Cathedral.

WOOD CROSS
XII
TRANI OR BOTTICINO MARBLE
2'.4"
CARVING WITH VENETIAN MOSAIC BACKGROUND OF SAME COLOR AS BACKGROUND OF FIGURES
BLACK OR BLUE BAKPIGLIO OR RED MARBLE BACKGROUND
FLORENTINE MARBLE MOSAIC FIGURES
JESUS DIES ON THE CROSS
INCISED INSCRIPTION PAINTED OF SAME COLOR AS BACKGROUND
3'.4"
Submitted by
CHICAGO OFFICE
85 East Delaware Place
SCALE 1" = 1 FT.

<u>FURNITURE & FIXTURES</u>

The following companies placed bids for the construction and furnishing of the church's sacristy furniture:

> The Tiffin Manufacturing Co.
> Church Furniture
> Tiffin, Ohio

> The Manitowoc Church Furniture Co.
> Waukesha, Wisconsin

> The Josephinum Church Furniture Co.
> Ecclesiastical Art Furniture
> 35-361 Merritt Street
> Columbus, Ohio

> Karl Hackert
> Church Interiors
> 25 East Delaware Place
> Chicago, Illinois

The Tiffin Manufacturing Co. of Tiffin, Ohio was awarded the contract for $3,953.00.[78] This contract included the following pieces of furniture:

> 5 Single Prie Dieus
> 1 Double Prie Dieus
> 7 Altar Boys Stools
> 2 Sanctuary Benches
> 1 Lectern
> 2 Credenza
> 3 Chaplain Stools

[79]

These pieces of furniture were to be made of white oak and hand carved with regards to the wood ornamentation.

The initial bids given were to include the Bishop's Throne and Sedillia but these two pieces were subsequently constructed of marble.

As with most of the work done at the Cathedral, there was delay in delivering these pieces of sacristy furniture. Mr. Schilling changed the finish staining color and was late in reporting these changes to the manufacturer.[80]

The candlesticks and crucifixes for the altars were designed and made by Karl Hackert, Church Interiors, 840 North Michigan Avenue, Chicago, Illinois. They were fabricated in bronze with a finish to match the tabernacle doors and bronze gates. The Corpus for the High Altar crucifix as well as on the other crucifixes may be wither silver oxidized or gold plated finish. The total amount paid for these fixtures was $2,595.00.[81]

LIST OF THE CONTRIBUTORS TO

THE REBUILDING OF THE

CATHEDRAL - 1936

Acme Electric Company
Ernest G. Anderson, Prop.
Electric Contractor & Dealer
Marquette, Michigan
$92.00

American Seating Company
Grand Rapids, Michigan
$6,739.75

American Steel Wire Co.
Chicago, Illinois
Steel Wire Rope

American Wire & Iron Works
Detroit, Michigan
2 ornamental steel constructed grilles
$354.00

Ammen Transfer Co.
Freight
$61.15

Andrew Anderson
Harold Anderson
Sand, Cement, Rock
$1,043.35

Atchison, Topeka & Santa Fe, RR Co.
Tulsa, Oaklahoma
Truscon Steel
$5.00

Automotive Sales & Service Inc.
Fond du Lac, Wisconsin
$32.23

Badger Wire & Iron Works
Milwaukee, Wisconsin
$5,342.00

Boucher's Drug Store
Marquette, Mich.
50¢

Bruumer & Lay
Chicago, Illinois
$20.00

Campbell Brothers
Marquette, Michigan
Sand, limestone, gravel
$1,345.25

The R. L. Carter Div.
New Britain, Conn.
Cutters, Grinding Wheels
$23.00

Carroll Motor Supply
Marquette, Michigan
$8.15

The Case Crane Co.
Columbus, Ohio
Wheelbarrows

H. Channon Company
Chicago, Illinois
$123.50

Chicago, Milwaukee, St. Paul &
Pacific RR Co.
$181.75

Chicago and North Western RR. Co.
$264.70

F. A. Chopper Iron Works
Detroit, Michigan
Circular Grilles
$305.00

Clover-Leaf Motor Truck Trans. Co.
Shipping
$1.20

W. D. Cochran Freight Lines
Iron Mountain, Michigan
$28.75

Consolidated Fuel & Lumber Co.
Marquette, Michigan
$4,253.35

H. J. Cronin's Drug Store
Negaunee, Michigan
$3.25

Arthur R. Cusick
Painting and Decorating
Marquette, Michigan
$130.00

Dallman & Cooper Supply Co.
Fond du Lac, Wisconsin
$2.75

Dayton Sure Grip & Stone
Dayton, Ohio
Wall Ties

Deluxe Check Printers
Chicago, Illinois
$2.00

Detroit Mantel & Tile Co.
Detroit, Michigan
Electric Fixtures
$6,921.60

Detroit Stained Glass Co.
Detroit, Michigan
$20,092.00

DiLorenzo Decorations
Architectual Decorator
Detroit, Michigan
$2,685.00

W. J. Drummond Co.
High Grade Stone & Metal Tools
Oshkosh, Wisconsin
$89.10

Duluth, South Shore & Atlantic RR Co.
Transportation to Marquette, Michigan
$283.75

J. L. Dunstone
Marquette, Michigan
$44.50

Dwyer & Trombley
Hardware & Housewares
Marquette, Michigan
$384.66

Electrical Administrative Board
Application for Electrical Inspection
State of Michigan
$2.00

T. C. Esses Co.
Milwaukee, Wisconsin
Stained Glass
$1,885.50

Flanigan Bros. Storage Co.
Marquette, Michigan
$2,138.85

John H. Freeman
Detroit, Michigan
$67.20

Gagnon Clay Products Co.
Green Bay, Wisconsin
$8,493.00

Gambles Stores
Marquette, Michigan
$25.75

General Supply Co.
Fond du Lac, Wisconsin
$6,791.42

Goldblatt Tool Co.
Kansa City, Mo.
$9.75

Grinnell Bros. Music House
Detroit, Michigan
Electric Work/Organ Installment
$66.20

Green Bay Pairing Co.
Green Bay, Wisconsin
$672.00

Phillip Gross Hardware Co.
Milwaukee, Wisconsin
$73.35

Guelff Printing Co.
Marquette, Michigan
10¢

P B. Haber Printing Co.
Fond du Lac, Wisconsin
$2.00

Hamiltion Natural Cut Stone Co.
Hamilton, Wisconsin
Flagstone
$52.50

Albert Hauer & Sons, Inc.
Painting & Decorating
Fond du Lac, Wisconsin
$1,652.35

S. C. Hemshat Co.
Lathing Service
Rochester, Minnesota
$2,340.60

Charles Horn
Expert Electrical Repairing
Fond du Lac, Wisconsin
$30.85

Horrigan Oil Company
Marquette, Michigan
$238.85

The Huber Brothers
Druggists, Booksellers, Stationers
Fond du Lac, Wisconsin
75¢

The Indian Hill Stone Co.
Bloomington, Indiana
Indiana Limestone
$9,533.48

Ingersall-Rand
New York, New York
Rivet Sets
$72.77

Insulation Service, Inc.
Milwaukee, Wisconsin
$1,850.00

The International Statuary & Altar Co.
Milwaukee, Wisconsin
$535.00

Kelly Hardware Co.
Marquette, Michigan
$2,389.80

Lake Shore Engine Works
Marquette, Michigan
$51.35

Lake Superior & Ishpeming RR Co.
$43.20

Lake Superior Ice Co.
Marquette, Michigan
$61.00

Lakeside Bridege & Steel Co.
Milwaukee, Wisconsin
Structural Steel
$10,488.72

Lakeside Iron Works
Machinists— Blacksmithing
Marquette, Michigan
$212.35

Lansing Co.
Lansing, Michigan
$2.00

E. C. Lemon
Portrait & Commercial Photographers
Marquette, Michigan
$27.00

Lency Clairmont Transfer
Milwaukee, Wisconsin
$43.87

Laeffler Iron Works
$23.00

A. A. Loehr Co.
Fond du Lac, Wisconsin
$67.15

R. Longtine
Marquette, Michigan
$170.00

Manitowoc Church Furniture Co.
Waukesha, Wisconsin

Manowski & Becker Co.
Fond du Lac, Wisconsin
$35.25

The Martin - Gibson Co.
Detroit, Michigan
$6,847.00

Marquette Pharmacy
Marquette, Michigan
$2.00

City of Marquette
Department of Light & Power
Marquette, Michigan
$328.62

Marquette Roofing & Sheet Metal Co.
Marquette, Michigan
$5,971.50

Meadowbrook Nursery
Landscaping & Tree Surgery
Marquette, Michigan
$3,408.60

The Michler Co.
Fond du Lac, Wisconsin
$23.25

Michigan Bell Telephone Co.
Saginaw, Michigan
$134.00

Milcor Steel Co.
Milwaukee, Wisconsin
$7.00

Millies Building Specialties Co.
Milwaukee, Wisconsin
$40.01

George Millward
General Blacksmithing
Marquette, Michigan
$47.15

Moore & Gallaway Lumber Co.
Fond du Lac, Wisconsin
$150.30

Morgan Company
Oshkosh, Wisconsin
Doors, Shelves, Stools
$7,334.44

Thomas Maulding Floor Co.
Chicago, Illinois
$453.00

Neenah Foundry Co.
Neenah, Wisconsin
$8.50

The Nichols Co.
Nichols Floor & Tile Co.
Detroit, Michigan
$2,975.00

Northern Terrazzo & Tile Co.
Negaunee, Michigan
$5,954.00

Northwestern Marble Corp.
Office and Marble Mill
Minneapolis, Minnesota
$45,335.00

Northwestern Terra Cotta Corp.
Chicago, Illinois
$9,040.00

W. J. Nuss Lumber & SupplyCo.
Fond du Lac, Wisconsin
$2.95

Pangborn Corporation
Hagerstown, Maryland
$310.75

Parducci STudio
Detroit, Michigan
$1,420.00

Patek Brothers, Inc.
MIlwaukee, Wisconsin
$12.75

Pendall Pharmacy
Marquette, Michigan
75¢

Peninsula Granite & Marble Co.
Marquette, Michigan
Marble Work
$109.50

Plumbers Supply Co.
Fond du Lac, Wisconsin
$47.89

U. S. Postal Service
Marquette, Michigan
$62.87

Public Service Garage
Marquette, Michigan
$17.80

Quality Hardware
Marquette, Michigan
75¢

Railway Express Agency, Inc.
Transportation
$134.50

Richard's Sport Shop
Marquette, Michigan
50¢

Rickeston Mineral Color Works
Milwaukee, Wisconsin
$154.35

Ross Lumber Co.
Chicago, Illinois
Yellow Pine
$1,053.50

Rossbach & Sons, Inc.
Ventilators, Frames & Domes
Chicago, Illinois
$4,512.37

M. Rossmiller
General Bandages, Inc.
$5.00

Joseph T. Ryerson & Son, Inc.
Iron – Steel – Machinery
Milwaukee, Wisconsin
$166.75

Sanitary Food Market
Marquette, Michigan
$3.50

Sanymetal Products Co.
Cleveland, Ohio
$146.50

Schnieder Bros. Lumber Co.
Marquette, Michigan
$3,698.93

Service Stamp Shop
Fond du Lac, Wisconsin
$1.30

Skilsaw Inc.
Chicago, Illinois
$26.50

The Soo – Marquette Hardware Co.
Marquette, Michigan
$12.17

F. B. Spear & Sons Building Mat.
Marquette, Michigan
$4,162.33

Stafford Drug Co.
Marquette, Michigan
$3.25

Stark Brick Co.
East Canton, Ohio
$61.00

Streator Brick Co.
Streator, Illinois
Brick
$177.25

Sport Shop Inc.
Fond du Lac, Wisconsin
$22.80

I. E. Swift Co.
Mining & Lumber Supplies
Houghton, Michigan
$85.75

Tiffin Manufacturing Co.
Sanctuary Furniture
$3,053.00

Tomassi Studios, Marble Art
New York, New York
$30,760

Tonella & Rupp Furniture
Marquette, Michigan
$1,572.25

Truscon Steel Co.
Youngstown, Ohio
Structural Steel
$1,905.58

Union National Bank
Marquette, Michigan
$5.75

U. P. Office Supply Co.
Marquette, Michigan
$21.00

Vollbrecht Cut Stone Company
Milwaukee, Wisconsin
$94.00

Vulcan Manufacturing Co.
Fond du Lac, Wisconsin
$29.95

Wadhams Oil Co.
Milwaukee, Wisconsin
$9.00

Washington St. Electric Shop
Marquette, Michigan
$2,943.15

Earl H. Werner
Painter & Decorator
Marquette, Michigan
$479.00

Wesley Freight Co.
Marinette, Wisconsin
$184.75

Western Union Co.
$36.00

Western Ornamental Co.
Milwaukee, Wisconsin
Ornamental plastering
$10,504.00

Woolworth Co.
Marquette, Michigan
5¢

REDECORATION OF THE CATHEDRAL IN 1947

In the Summer of 1947 it was decided to redecorate the Cathedral
and place a mural on the back sacristy wall. Also, painting of the sacristy
ceiling and side walls would be included in this redecoration.

This work had previously been released for bids in 1937 and the
following companies were recontacted regarding their previous proposals:

> Arthur Hercz Studios
> 1401 North Park Avenue
> Chicago, Illinois
>
> Joseph F. Falkenbach
> Ecclesiastical Artist
> 125 E. Wells Street
> Milwaukee, Wisconsin
>
> Karl Hackert
> Church Interiors
> 25 East Delaware Place
> Chicago, Illinois

The bid was given to Karl Hackert for the proposed sum of $10,000.00.[82]

The specifications and estimates were as follows:

SCOPE OF WORK:

The work covered by this specification consists of the furnishing of all labor, materials and equipment, excluding the
scaffolding, for the complete painting and decorating of all
plaster surfaces of the interior of Saint Peter's Cathedral:
the Cathedral proper, the vestibules, stairs, passages, gallery
and sacristies and Bishop's Chapel.

PREPARATION:

Dropcloths and paper shall be spread wherever painting and
decorating are being done. All plaster patching normally
done by painters shall be part of this contract.

All surfaces are to be cleaned. No surfaces shall be painted
and decorated that are not in every respect sound and ready
to receive paint. New plaster patches shall be treated with
zinc sulphate.

MATERIALS:

All materials to be used shall be the best of their respective
kinds. After close inspection of the walls and the ceiling,
the materials best suited to finish these surfaces shall be
selected and applied.

TREATMENT:

The decoration of the Sanctuary wall of the Cathedral shall
follow, in general, the sketch submitted, or Sketch "B"
enclosed. All halos and the vesica around the figure of our
Lord shall be executed in genuine gold leaf; the background
shall be executed in metal leaf, as shown on the sketch previously submitted, or in color as indicated on Sketch "B".

A sample figure shall be submitted, first in the form of a
charcoal drawing, then completely painted and studied for
size and effect.

Special studies for the decoration of the Sanctuary ceiling,
which is to be treated in ornamental design, shall be submitted for approval. Full size samples shall be made thereafter
for the Sanctuary ceiling and again submitted for approval.

No final mural nor decorative work shall proceed until all
samples have been approved.

The decoration now existing in the Cathedral shall be cleaned
and touched up.

INSURANCES:

I carry Unemployment and Occupational disease insurances;
also, workmen's compensation insurances for full statutory
requirements and manufacturers and contractors (contingent)
public liability and property damage, completed operations
coverage, public liability and property damage with limits
on all public liability of $100,000.00 for each person and
$300,000.00 for each accident. Limit of liability for all prop-
erty damage of $5,000.00 for each accident. Certificate of
insurance shall be furnished before the work proceeds.

START AND COMPLETION:

The work is to be started on or about October fifteen and is
to be completed as early as possible in December, barring
strikes, lockouts and other conditions beyond our control.

PRICE:

The total cost of all the work specified will be TEN THOUSAND
DOLLARS ($10,000.00). It is understood that half of this amount

is accounted for by the painting and decorating of the
Sanctuary wall and ceiling; the other half of the work shall
be done on a cost-plus basis, figuring 15% for overhead and
10% for profit, and guaranteed not to exceed Five Thousand
Dollars ($5,000).

83

The description of the mural on the background of the sacristy was:

"Under this scheme we suggest placing against a gold background, the figure of Christ standing with His right hand
raised, holding in His left hand the silver and gold Keys,
handing them down to St. Peter, symbolizing the conferring
of the gift of infallibility upon His first Vicar, the chief
of the Apostles. To the right and left are the eleven other
apostles, each shown with his proper emblem. The appropriate
inscription might read: 'Tu es Petrus et super hanc petram
aedificabo ecclesiam meam, et portae inferi non praevalebunt
adversus eam; et tibi dabo claves regni coelorum. Alleluia!'

The angels above, one on each side of the figure of Christ,
hold replicas, the one of St. Peter's in Rome, the other of
St. Peter's in Marquette."

84

As in most redecoration or construction work there are cost over-runs
that are unexpected by the people doing the work and those paying for the work.
This was also the case in the redecoration of the Cathedral. Apparently,
the accoustical tile on the ceiling required more work than initially estimated
and one of the foremen became overzealous in the Bishop's Chapel restoration:

"At the time I submitted this proposal to you, you inquired
whether or not the Bishop's Chapel had been included and I
replied that it was not, but that I would try to do it as part
of the work in the Cathedral proper. As you know, the contract called for 'Painting and decorating of all plaster surfaces
of the interior of St. Peter's Cathedral: the Cathedral proper,
the vestibules, stairs, passages, gallery and sacristies.'

In return for my readiness to include the Bishop's Chapel, you
assured me that if we should not come out all right on the
entire job, you would be willing to make up for it.

As you know, the cleaning of the ceiling of the Cathedral

-53-

presented unexpected difficulties which one could not foresee.
In addition, the progress of the work was repeatedly delayed
on account of insufficient scaffolding and scaffolding not
ready when we needed it. This required repeated laying off
and taking on of a number of men which considerably decreased
the efficiency of the work. Due to the willingness of our foreman
to follow your suggestion and clean the marble wainscot in the
Bishop's Chapel, we met with some difficulty and we went
to considerable expense in restoring the finish.

I feel sure that you would want us to present this matter as
it actually stands. I shall be grateful for your consideration
of these facts."

[85]

This, of course, was resolved for the total sum of $704.00 which essentially

paid for the time invested by the workers.[86]

This was the final chapter, other than routine cleaning, for any redecorating

of the Cathedral until the Fall of 1980. At that time, it was decided to re-

decorate and liturgically update the Cathedral beginning in January, 1981.

TOUR GUIDE OF ST. PETER'S CATHEDRAL - 1981

The exterior walls of this beautiful Cathedral are made of native Marquette

sandstone. The walls were originally constructed in 1881 and remained after

the fire of 1935 which virtually destroyed the entire roof and complete interior.

As you look up at the steeples, you will see the lower portion constructed

of sandstone and the upper portion of brownstone. The domes, which are red,

blue and orange, adorn the top of these steeples and a cross of gold leaf sits

on each dome. Copper eaves form the edging on the roof of the church and

on the peak of this copper eave is a cross made of steel.

As you look at the entrance doors of the Cathedral, you will see high

above them, statues of two apostles, St. Peter, on your left, and St. Paul,

on your right. The Diocese Coat of Arms with angels on each side is beneath

these statues. As you look at the large, oak entrance doors, the left door has

an anchor above it, which represents hope, the center door has a cross and

crown above it, which represents faith, and the right door has a heart above

it, which represents love. To the left of these doors is the original corner-

stone showing Bishop Baraga's Coat of Arms and the date 1881, A.D..

As you enter into the foyer of the Cathedral, the stairs to the left ascend

to the choir loft. If you ascend these stairs you will see a stained glass

window of an angel holding a replica of St. Peter's Cathedral.

To the right of the foyer, is the priest's sacristy where the garments

are kept to celebrate Mass. In the foyer you can see brass rails, sculpted

plaster with gold gilt and the oak doors leading into the main church. As

you go through these oak doors, move forward and turn around. Standing here,

look up at the choir loft which is constructed of oak. Originally, the entire

choir loft was to be constructed of oak but it was decided to construct the

floor of reinforced steel and concrete and then oak boarding was added to
this substructure.

As you look at the entrance doors, above the center door is the Coat of
Arms of the Papacy, above the left door is the Coat of Arms of Bishop Baraga
and above the right door is the Coat of Arms of Bishop Schmitt and the Diocese.
The Coat of Arms of Bishop Plagens was here previously as he was the Bishop
at the time of the 1935 construction, but it was replaced by Bishop Schmitt's
Coat of Arms as he was the Diocese Head during the 1981 renovation.

Looking up, the ceiling is approximately 67 feet in height from the floor.
The tiles are approximately $1\frac{1}{2}'$ by $\frac{1}{2}'$. Now, as you turn and look into the
main church, you see this ceiling is supported by 24 Romanesque pillars which
are faced with red Scagiola marble. This is not real marble but rather a mixture of marble powder and a plaster-like substance. You will also see four
sqaure pillars which are faced with polished mankato stone. These pillars
were added when the church was rebuilt to support the roof of such a great
height. You will also notice that the walls inside this church are constructed
of polished mankato stone.

Proceed up the center aisle and look at the impressiveness of the 24
marble columns. As you walk up the aisle, look at the floor which is most unique.
Mad of natural red clay, the mosaic-like floor is interspersed with tile adorned
with the symbol of Christian antiquity, Chi Rho, the Greek letters signifying
the name of Christ Jesus.

As you look to your right and left, there are beautiful stained glass
windows. On your right, the stained glass windows represent the mysteries
of the rosary which are aspects of the Life of Christ. The top panels represent
the Glorious Mysteries and from the back, going forward, we see the Coronation

of the Blessed Mother, the Assumption, the Descent of the Holy Spirit, the
Ascension, and the Resurrection. The middle panels represent the Sorrowful
Mysteries, from the back forward, the Crucifixion, Jesus carries the cross
and meets His mother, the Crowning with Thorns, the Scourging, and the Agony
in the Garden. In the lower panels are the Joyful Mysteries, from the back
forward they are: the Finding of the Child Jesus in the Temple, the Presentation,
the Nativity, the Visitation, and the Annunciation. You will also notice
"little extras" in these windows which are symbols, again from Christian
antiquity. The stained glass windows to the left depict five of the Saints,
scenes from the Life of Christ, and other ceremonial occurrences of the
Catholic faith. The top panels, from back to front, depict St. Joseph, the
father of Jesus, St. Boniface, St. Patrick, patron Saint of Ireland, St. Stanislaus,
and St. John the Baptist. The middle panels show the Betrothal of Mary and
Joseph, the Coronation of a King, St. Patrick ridding Ireland of snakes, the
Apparition of the Blessed Virgin Mary and the Christ Child to St. Stanislaus
and finally, the Baptism of Jesus by St. John. The lower panels, from back
forward, show St. Joseph and Mary teaching Jesus, the laying of the foundation
of the Church, St. Patrick and two kings, an Angel giving Communion to a
saint and St. John preaching to the people.

As you stand in the middle of the church, look at the large transept
windows. The west transept window, is the Mother, Queen of Heaven window.
In the center uppermost part, Mary, the Queen, is surrounded with Angels
and Cherubs encircles the Symbols of Mary: the Gate of Heaven, a Star
and Crescent, Flur de lys and the Pierced Heart. Below these are the other
six Apostles: St. Thomas, St. Paul, St. James Major, St. Jude, St. Simon and
St. Matthias also distinguished by their symbols which have been placed above

them. Below these figures are Symbols of Mary: a Fountain, the Ave Maria and the Anchor. To the right of this transept window is a smaller window, displaying on the top, St. John, represented by an eagle, in the middle, St. John holding a chalice and the host and on the bottom, the Sacrament of the Sick. To the left of this transept window, the smaller window depicts at the top, St. Luke, who is represented by an ox, in the middle, St. Luke holding an axe and the lower panel shows the Sacrament of Marriage.

The east transept window, to the left, is the Christ the King window. This large window contains in the center uppermost part, Christ the King, surrounded with Angels and Cherubs encircled with Symbols of Christ: the Alpha and Omega, Chi Rho, X.P. and I.H.C.. Below these are the six Apostles, St. James Minor, St. Peter, St. John, St. Andrew, St. Bartholemew and St. Phillip each known by their symbol which is interwoven in the glass above each figure. Below these figures are the Symbols of Christ: the Chalice, Agnus Dei and the Font. The window to the right of this transept window shows St. Mark repre- sented by a lion, at the top, St. Mark holding a tree in the middle, and the Sacrament of Confirmation at the bottom. The window to the left of the large transept window shows at the top, St. Matthew represented by an angel, St. Matthew holding a quill and a book in the middle, and the Sacrament of Baptism at the bottom. If you turn around and look up at the choir loft you will see three windows containing four single figures of the musical saints: St. Cecilia, St. Ambrose, St. David and St. Gregory. Single figures of five adoring angels with musical instruments - trumpet, cymbals, drum and triangle are also present. The Dove of the Holy Spirit is placed in the top of the center window and symbols of Christ in the bottom of the window.

As you are in the middle of church now, look to the East and you will see the side altar shrine which is dedicated to the Sacred Heart. This shrine

represents Jesus giving His Sacred Heart to St. Margaret Mary Aloquet. This

is an expression symbolic of the divine love that the Master has for all of His

children no matter who they are or where they may be. It is His heart which

sheds the blood given for the salvation of all people. Without that life-giving

source we would be nothing but dust.

To the west you will see the Shrine of St. Anne, the mother of Mary.

Devotion to St. Anne grew quite popular in the 14th Century, A.D.. Stories

recount how St. Anne was visited by an angel, told of the birth of Mary, and

how great a part her daughter was to play in the history of salvation.

These shrines and their statues along the side aisles are executed in solid,

natural colored marbles, acquired in many lands, untouched by stains or arti-

ficial tints. These marbles were carved separately and in the Saints' traditional

colors, then fitted together so that no joints are seen.

Going forward, you will see the main altar of celebration. The high

altar, which was behind the Bishop's chair in front of you, was used in previous

times for the celebration of Mass. With the new changes in the Liturgy, the

priest now faces the people and is worshipping in community. To the right of

the altar is the baptistry. You will notice the six columns that support this

baptistry are made of three different designs. These columns came from the

marble of the old High Altar which was dismantled during the 1981 renovation.

Off to the right, in the recess of the wall, are kept the Holy Oils used

in various Catholic ceremonies and institution of the Sacraments.

To the right of the sanctuary is the statue of St. Joseph, carpenter and

foster father of Jesus and to the left of the sanctuary, the statue of St. Mary

the Virgin Mother of God. These statues again display the intricate marble design of the 1930's. You will notice the arches over these statues. They are

composed of Pewabic tile. This tile was originally fabricated in the Upper

Peninsula and is no longer commercially available. The votive lights in the front

of the statues are lit as a symbol of prayers or special requests to these Saints.

As you proceed up and behind the main altar you see the Bishop's chair.

The Bishop's chair was originally designed for Bishop Plagens who was the

Bishop in residence when the church was rebuilt in 1935. This chair is the

Bishop's chair when he presides at any celebration in this church. Only the

Bishop may sit in this chair. The Bishop's chair also signifies that St. Peter's

Cathedral is the Mother Church of the Diocese.

If you look up at the mural which is on the back wall of the sanctuary,

you will see a representative painting of Christ giving the keys of Heaven

to St. Peter. To the right is an angel holding a representation of St. Peter's

Basilica in Rome. The connection between them is that St. Peter's Cathedral

in Marquette is the Mother Church for Catholics of the Diocese of Marquette

and the St. Peter's Basilica in Rome is the Mother Church for Catholics of

the world. You will also notice the figures of the eleven remaining Apostles.

The Apostles are: St. James the Less, St. Andrew, St. Bartholemew, St. Phillip,

St. Jude, St. James the Greater, St. John, St. Matthew, St. Mathais, St. Thomas

and St. Simon. Beneath the Apostles notice the sheep present and the Latin

phrase which, translated, reads:

> "You are Peter, and upon this rock I will build my church,
> and the gates of hell shall not prevail against it. To you I
> give the keys to the kingdom of Heaven. Alleluia!"

This phrase is taken from the Gospel of St. Matthew, Chapter 16:13-19.

The total richness that this mural portrays bespeaks almost of an icon. Icons

were used by worshipers to represent saints before the appearance of statues.

The characteristics of icons are very evident here in this most beautiful mural.

Proceed from the sanctuary to the side entrance and Chapel of the Blessed Sacrament. Before you enter through this door, look above you. You will see a white marble-framed Venetian mosaic which represents one of the 14 stations of the Cross. These 14 stations represent the Way of the Cross and are on the side walls of the Church.

As you proceed through these doors to the entrance of the Chapel of the Blessed Sacrament, directly in front of you, is the lovely Shrine of the Little Flower. The pedestal is richly carved red brocato marble and Italian brown onyx. The cloak of St. Theresa is of ivory-colored Tranny marble, the tunicle of brown Italian onyx, the cross and veil are carved of Belgian black marble and the delicate, flesh portions are made of onyx from Portugal. All of the marble and mosaic pieces you are seeing in the church were done by Giuseppe Tommasi studios with main offices located in Carrara, Italy.

Going into the Chapel of the Blessed Sacrament you will notice the stained glass windows on each side. These stained glass windows represent the first six Bishops of the Catholic Church. The windows on the left represent St. Martin, St. Francis, and St. Chrysostom. The windows to the right depict St. Stanislaus, St. Alphonsus and St. Augustine. This Chapel previously was named the Bishop's Chapel but after the renovation it was retitled the Chapel of the Blessed Sacrament as the Holy Eucharist is reposed in its sanctuary.

The Bishop's Chapel, now the Chapel of the Blessed Sacrament, was an addition to the original rebuilding plans of the Cathedral in 1935. It was added so the Bishop would have his own private chapel in which to celebrate Mass. As you go to the front of the Chapel, you again see Pewabic tile on the steps and you will notice on your right a statue of St. Anthony of Padua and to the left a marble shrine with an icon of Our Lady of Perpetual Help. It is believed that St. Luke, physician and evangelist, painted the original from which this document is made. As you look to the front of the chapel, you will see an exquisite Venetian mosaic panel above the tabernacle. This mosaic is of Christ the King. There are two children at Christ's feet, and He is surrounded by six Cherubim. On the walls to each side of the mosaic are six angels, three on each side, bearing shields with symbols of our Lord's passion. The mural on the back wall represents the Paschal Lamb of God above which is the Holy Spirit represented by a dove. Encircling the Paschal Lamb and Holy Spirit are the Cherubim with angels at the lower right and left corners. As you leave the Chapel you will notice pictures on the side and back walls. These pictures are of the Bishops that have served the Diocese of Marquette. In order they are: Baraga, Mrak, Vertin, Eis, Nussbaum, Plagens, Magner, Noa and Salatka. Therefore, in the history of the Cathedral of Marquette, we have had nine previous Bishops, with Bishop Schmitt being the tenth Bishop in residence.

Now you may proceed downstairs to view the burial vaults of Bishop Baraga and five other Bishops: Mrak, Vertin, Eis, Magner and Noa. Entering the crypt you will find prayer cards to Bishop Baraga and a place to kneel and pray for the Lord's help through the Intercession of Bishop Baraga. His Cause for Canonization is currently being processed and presented to the Congregation of Saints in Rome.

With this invitation for private prayer, we fittingly conclude our tour of the Cathedral. You may feel free to browse around and further enjoy the beauty and splendor of this lovely Cathedral dedicated to the Apostle, St. Peter.

87, 88, 89, 90, 91, 92

TABLES

TABLE I

REQUEST FOR PAYMENT
(INITIAL ESTIMATE)

FROM

THE HUTTER CONSTRUCTION COMPANY

REQUEST FOR PAYMENT

Hutter Construction Co.

Fond du Lac, Wis.

August 24, 1938

Contract No. 3625

Project: St. Peter's Cathedral

Location: Marquette, MI.

Architect: Edward A. Schilling

Contract For: General Construction

Items	Values
General Conditions	$ 3,360.00
Demolition – Excavating	2,882.34
Concrete Footings	1,372.00
Concrete Walls	1,195.25
Concrete Columns, Beams & Fireproofing	1,754.11
Concrete Slabs	1,662.28
Concrete Formwork	1,849.40
Cement Floor and Walks	2,654.92
Alterations – Boiler Room	282.32
Cut Stone	13,500.00
Interior Stone	14,439.00
Face Brick	1,985.92
Terra Cotta	9,050.00
Scaffolding	3,448.94
Masonry and Back-up	23,067.14
Miscellaneous Masonry Items	6,544.41
Carpentry	15,426.21
Lath and Plaster	27,668.09
Tile Work	3,018.00
Gibraltar Floors & Terrazzo	3,113.48
Lineleum	1,152.30
Structural Steel	18,640.00
Steel Joist & Lath	3,200.00
Miscellaneous & Ornamental Iron	4,983.00
Reinforcing	1,495.81
Vault Door & Fireproof Door	250.00
Steel Sash	4,348.04
Sheet Metal & Roofing	6,157.00
Caulking	137.88
Glass & Glazing	1,491.00
Painting	1,275.00
Models & Carving	2,000.00
Brown Stone Work	17,500.00
Insurance	4,696.16
Job Overhead	3,600.00
	$211,000.00
Service Charge	20,000.00
LIMIT OF COST	$231,000.00

TABLE II

GENERAL CONTRACTOR SPECIFICATIONS

<u>GENERAL CONTRACTOR</u>

<u>THE GENERAL CONDITIONS IN THE FRONT OF THESE SPECIFICATIONS
TOGETHER WITH THE FOLLOWING GOVERN THIS WORK.</u>

<u>PROPOSALS</u>
Sealed Proposals for the following work will be received by __________
not later than __________________________.
Proposals shall be marked on the outside of the envelope with the
name of the bidder and "PROPOSAL FOR ST. PETER'S CATHEDRAL,
MARQUETTE, MICHIGAN".

<u>CLAIMS</u>
Any claim of one contractor against another on this building shall be
made in writing within four days of the occurrence of the cause of such
claim. An itemized invoice in duplicate shall be prepared, one copy of which
shall be filed immediately upon completion of the operation, with the contractor against whom the claim is made, and another copy with the Architect,
or the claim will not be recognized.

<u>PLANS AND SPECIFICATIONS</u>
These shall be used together. Notes and indications on drawings are
equal in value to mention in specifications.
If question arises concerning plans and specifications, or omissions are
found, they are to be immediately brought to the attention of the Architect
for clarification and revision.
Each contractor shall read over the specifications referring to the work
of other trades adjoining his, and he shall assist all other contractors in
securing a good job, insofar as they are dependent on each other.

<u>DUTIES OF THE CLERK OF WORKS</u>
The office of the Clerk of the Works is to looks after the Owner's
interests, and his presence shall in no way relieve the contractor from
responsibility for the proper execution of any and all details of the construction
of the building. The Contractor shall afford the Clerk of Works all possible
opportunity to inspect the work and materials. All work incorrectly executed
shall be immediately corrected, and condemned material shall be promptly
removed from the premises. The fact that faulty workmanship or materials
have escaped detection in no way releases the contractor from responsibility,
nor will it prevent rejection at a future time.

<u>"APPROVED" OR "EQUAL"</u>
In these specifications the words "approved" and "or equal" are intended
to cover the best articles of their kind, and should the contractor desire to
substitute material of "equal" quality in place of the particular material
specified, he must submit a sample of such material and must receive the
Architect's approval of same in writing before ordering any of the said
material.

-1-

WORK INCLUDED
    One General Contract shall include all labor and material specified
immediately following particular headings, and also all labor and materials
called for under the gollowing general headings:
    (A) Masonry and Brickwork, including reinforced concred and rein-
         forcing steel.
    (B) Cut Stone complete
    (C) Iron and Steel Work (Structural)
    (D) Miscellaneous Iron Work
    (E) Roofing and Sheet Metal Work
    (F) Lathing and Plastering
    (G) Carpentry and Joinery
    (H) Marble, tile and terrazzo work
    (I) Painting
    (J) Glazing

TELEPHONE
    This Contractor shall cause to be installed in proper place at job,
at beginning of operations, a Michigan State Telephone for use of all Contractors
and the Architect, and shall pay for service of same until the building is
completed and accepted by the Owner.

PERMITS
    This Contractor shall obtain and pay for all Public Permits and Approvals
as necessary to complete his work except building permit which shall be
obtained by Owner.

LEVELS AND LINES
    All lines, levels, angles and batter boards needed to properly locate
new parts of building shall be established by a competent man with approved
level and transit, to the entire satisfaction of the Architect, before proceeding
with any work.

PROTECTICN OF PUBLIC
    The Contractor shall exercise all due precaution to insure the safety
of the public and shall build and maintain a fence enclosure on all sides
necessary, as directed. No bills shall be allowed on fence.

PROTECTION OF TREES
    All existing trees and shrubbery shall be protected in substantial fashion
with boards or wire netting.

OFFICE
    This Contractor shall erect in location on lot as directed or agreed
upon, a suitable frame building for use as a job office and Clerk of the
Works' office. Same shall be kept well off the ground and shall have suitable windows and doors.
    Door shall be well secured with a lock. Furnish Architect with a key
to same.
    Building shall be thoroughly weather-proof, well lighted and heated in

winter weather. Build approved desk space and plan rack. Rack shall be
so placed that plans on same will conform with the direction of the main
building.

STORAGE

Build water-proof shed with floor raised for storage of cement, lime,
tools, etc., of all workmen.

TEMPORARY CONVENIENCE

This Contractor shall build at beginning of his work a suitable earth
closet for the use of all workmen. He shall maintain same in decent and
sanitary condition removing the contents from time to time, and disinfecting
with quick lime, and when directed shall remove the whole from the job,
including all contaminated soil or material, replacing with fresh clean material
and scattering quick lime over the site. If connections are available, this
may be located in basement of present building.

SCAFFOLDING

Each Contractor shall furnish, erect, and maintain all scaffolding,
ladders, etc., as necessary for the progress of his own work.

SUB-CONTRACTOR

The names of all sub-contractors proposed to be employed shall be
submitted with the tender for the approval of the Architect. The Architect
reserves the right to reject any sub-contractor who is not deemed to be up
to the standard of work.

The work required of each sub-contractor shall be the work described
in his sub-division of the specification and shall be performed for the General
Contractor in the same manner as though he were a principal in the contract.

All transactions with the sub-contractors shall be made through the
General Contractor, except incidental items that may arise on the job.

REMOVING RUBBISH

All rubbish and refuge materials for all parts of the operations of all
trades included under this contract shall be removed from time to time,
as directed, from the building and the site, by this Contractor, all being
left in a clear and neat condition at completion.

Cost of cleaning shall be charged back as the various sub-contractors
in proportions as agreed at time of signing sub-contractors! contracts.

FOREMAN

This Contractor shall employ a fully competent foreman as approved
by the Architct, to superintend all parts of the work and fit the different
trades together. It will be his duty to secure from the architects all necessary details for all trades and he will be responsible for the progress of
the work.

PROGRESS SCHEDULE

Before signing the contract, this contractor shall file with the Architect
a full and itemized schedule of all dates at which different stages of work
will be completed. To maintain this schedule the contractors shall work
such overtime as may be necessary without extra charge.

PRICE SCHEDULE

Before contract is awarded the General Contractor shall furnish the Architect a price schedule of the various items entering into the contract, and as may be required by the Architect, which schedule shall be used as a basis for the making of Estimates of payment by the Architect in favor of the Contractor.

CONTRACTOR'S MEETINGS

Once every two weeks, when directed, there shall be held at the job office a meeting of the representatives of all trades at that time employed on the building, for furthering the progress of the building operations and the giving of instructions by the Architect's Superintendent and the General Contractor.

These meetings shall be presided over, directed, and called by the General Contractor's Cuperintendent, and he shall be responsible to the Architect for the regularity and attendance.

Contractors' representatives failing to attend these meetings when properly notified in writing by the Contractor's Superintendent, or by the Architect, shall be dismissed from the job and replaced by others.

TEMPORARY HEAT

The General Contractor shall furnish all necessary heat to maintain a proper temperature within the building after it is closed in, and until it is taken over by the Owner, not less than 60 degrees Fahrenheit during the period of plastering, and after plastering during the period of finishing by the Carpenter and Painter.

Heating system, including boiler piping and temporary radiation will be installed as soon as possible by the heating contractor, and will then be taken over by the General Contractor who will be responsible for its care and maintenance and full cost.

Previous to this installation the General Contractor shall furnish the heat by means of approved salamanders, etc. Cost and maintenance of same shall be charged back to the sub-contractors as before specified under "REMOVING RUBBISH".

TEMPORARY LIGHTING & POWER

The General Contractor shall pay for all permits, wiring, sockets, globes, service, etc., for all temporary lighting for all trades included under this contract.

Cost and maintenance of same shall be charged back to the sub-contractors as before specified under "REMOVAL OF RUBBISH".

WATER

The Plumbing Contractor will take out and pay for permit, and will bring service pipe to a convenient position, but the General Contractor shall pay City Charges for all water required by himself, and his sub-contractors. A proportion of the cost of this shall be charged back to sub-contractors as before specified under "REMOVING RUBBISH".

Water supply may be had from supply now on the site. This contractor shall provide and maintain suitable pump for the use of all sub-contractors on the job, if such is necessary.

FULL SIZE DETAILS

The General Contractor and each and every sub-contractor shall make requests in writing to the Architets for all full size details as necessary and not shown on the plans or specified, in ample time to prevent holding up the progress of his work, or the work of others and at least three weeks previous to the time he will need some.

Within five (5) days after receipt of details, each Contractor shall, in writing, to the Architect, protest against any parts of said details that he may consider as incurring additional work.

Unless the protest be made within the time named, the work shall be executed as detailed.

DAMAGE

Each Contractor shall be held responsible by the General Contractor for all damage caused by his work or workmen, to the plaster, woodwork, glass, painter's finish, and to all other work or material done by any other contractor. Patching and replacing of damaged work shall be done by Contractor who furnished the materials and performed the labor as directed by the Architect; the cost of replacement shall be paid for by the Contractor who is responsible for the damage. The General Contractor shall assume full responsibility for the proper adjustment of those items and settle same without recourse to Owner and to satisfaction of Architect or his representative.

If the evidence is insufficient, in the opinion of the Architect, to fix liability, the cost of such replacement shall be borne by all contractors employed on the job in amounts proportionate to the amounts of their respective contracts.

ACCELERATION OF WORK

If any part of the work needs to be finished in advance of other parts of the work, all contractors shall concentrate their men on such work as the Architect may direct.

MASONRY ETC.

<u>THE GENERAL CONDITIONS AND GENERAL CONTRACTOR'S SPECIFICA-
TION IN THE FRONT OF THESE SPECIFICATIONS TOGETHER WITH THE
FOLLOWING TO GOVERN THIS WORK.</u>

DEMOLITION

Remove all unnecessary masonry work of the existing building, laying
aside all materials for future use that may be re-used. Any materials arising
from this demolition and which may be found to be good and suitable may
be used in the new work, subject to the approval of the Architect. Old
brick and stone shall be thoroughly cleaned before being used. All materials
not suitable for the new work, or rejected by the Architect shall become the
property of the Contractor and shall be removed from the job.

ADDITION & ALTERATION TO EXISTING BUILDING

This Contractor shall do all excavation required for the addition and
alteration of the existing building, cut or remove all old masonry and make
all masonry alterations to the existing structure as shown on drawings and
as required by the nature of the work. He shall bond all new work thoroughly
into old at every alternate course of brick or stone, cut new openings in old
wall where shown, build up openings shown to be built up, cut bearings for
beams, etc. All new work shall be laid up in cement mortar.

CURBING & SHORING

This Contractor shall provide all necessary curbing and shoring required
to maintain the new excavations and prevent banks from slipping, and shall
do all necessary strutting or supporting necessary to maintain existing work
until permanent construction is installed. This Contractor shall take all
necessary precautions to ensure the safety of the existing buildings, shall be
responsible for its safety and shall make good at his own expense any damage
caused by his operations.

UNDERPINNING

This Contractor shall execute any underpinning required, using concrete
as hereafter specified for foundations, or hard burned common brick in cement
mortar. Underpinning shall be done in sections not exceeding three feet in
length, each section bonded thoroughly to the adjacent sections.

BACKFILLING & GRADING

This Contractor shall do all backfilling and grading required. Backfilling shall consist of at least 12" of broken brick stone or gravel above the
footing drains, remainder of excavated material, thoroughly tamped. Grade
around new building as indicated on drawings and corresponding with existing
grades, using black loam only for topping. Any building rubbish used for
backfill must be covered with at least 24" of clean soil.

FOOTING & CROCK DRAINS

Extend the existing 4" agricultural tile drains round new outside walls
and lay all new crock drains of sizes and as shown on plans, and make all

necessary connections to existing drains or sewer. All drains passing through
foundations shall be Cast Iron and footing drains shall be covered with tar
paper wt. not less than 15 lbs. per square.

Drain pipe shall be of the best vitrified salt glazed type, sizes as marked
on plans. They shall be bedded on the solid ground, cutting out for hubs.
Joints shall be thoroughly caulked with oakum and cemented. Inside joints
shall be thoroughly swabbed out as drains are laid.

Drains shall be laid in straight lengths, properly graded by means of a
spirit level. All changes of direction shall be gradual, using proper bends
and curves. At all changes of direction a hand hole shall be placed, brought
up to the surface and finished with cast iron screwed cleanout, with brass
slotted floor plug flush with floor.

All open ends left for connections of floor traps shall be carefully
plugged with burlap, fastened in such fashion that it cannot be pushed into
the drains.

TRAP PIT

Build Trap Pit of brick in cement mortar as shown, with 5" concrete
floor and concrete top reinforced as directed.

Set frame and manhole cover as supplied by others.

STONE, SPLASH BORDER AT GRADE

At the Grade provide a 26" broken stone border around entire building
to receive the rainwater from roof. This border is to be properly graded to
sumps connected to drain tile lines. This border is to be built with a 4"
concrete base and finished with 1" cement top smoothly trowelled to make a
proper finish (See plat plan) stone on premises.

PROTECTION OF BASEMENT & FOOTINGS

Basement bottom and footings of all walls shall be protected from weather
or damage at all times by a sufficiency of manure or other frost preventative,
to insure full protection against frost.

Should any settlement occur, this contractor shall be held responsible
for same and shall make same good at his own expense.

SAND

Sand shall be thoroughly clean and sharp, uniformly graded from fine
to coarse with coarse predominating, and shall contain not over three per cent
(3%) of loam or other impurities.

Samples shall be submitted to the Clerk of Works for his approval and
all sand used shall be equal to the approved sample.

CEMENT

Cement unless otherwise specified shall be American Portland subject
to tests as hereafter specified for REINFORCED CONCRETE.

Non-staining Cement shall be Atlas White or other equal approved brand.

LIME

Lime shall be hydrated, "Tiger Brand" or other approved equal manufacture. It shall be soaked in the mortar pan for not less than twenty-
four (24) hours before use, with clean water in proportions of about sixteen

(16) gallons of water per one hundred pounds (100#) of lime.

MORTARS
All mortars shall be thoroughly mixed in accordance with the best practice.

Cement and gauged mortars shall be mixed in small quantities for immediate use and any which has begun to set, or which has stood longer than one hour shall not be used.

CEMENT MORTAR shall consist of one part Portland Cement and two parts sand, and unless otherwise specified may be tempered with not exceeding ten per cent (10%) of lime. For non-bearing interior partition work the proportion of sand may be increased to three parts.

LIME MORTAR shall consist of one part lime and three parts sand.

GAUGED MORTAR shall consist of one part cement and three parts lime mortar.

Where so specified, non-staining cement shall be substituted for Portland in any of the above mortars.

REINFORCED CONCRETE & REINFORCING STEEL
All new footings, Foundation walls and retaining walls to grade level, or to the extent shown on drawings, the walls and roofs or floors of all pits, pipe tunnels or underfloor ducts, and new floors shall be of concrete, and shall be reinforced as shown on drawings and as hereafter specified.

SYSTEM
The system of reinforcing is shown on the framing plans of the Architect's drawings.

Any one of the standard patented systems may be used. IN case a patented system is to be used, the said system must be submitted to the Architect for his approval and the steel areas required by the Architects drawings must be maintained.

PROTECTION OF WORK AND PROPERTY
The Contractor shall continuously maintain adequate protection of all his work from damage and shall protect the Owner's property from injury or loss arising in connection with this Contract. He shall make good any such damage, injury or loss, except such as may be directly due to errors in the Contract Documents or caused by agents or employees of the Owner. He shall adequately protect adjacent property as provided by law and the Contract Documents. He shall provide and maintain all passage ways, guard fences, lights and other facilities for protection required by public authority or local conditions.

He shall provide proper facilities at all times for the inspection by the Architect, the Superintendent, and shall furnish, when required, test cubes 6" in size, made from the regular mixture used in the work. These cubes shall be tested by a laboratory as approved by the Architect or the Owner at the expense of this contractor.

LOCAL REGULATIONS
All above reinforced concrete work shall be built in accordance with these specifications and the accompanying drawings and shall comply with the requirements of the Local Department of Buildings.

The said laws shall be considered as a part of these specification, as though written herein.

DRAWINGS

Provide and submit for the approval of the Architect complete field drawings, showing the size of the reinforcing steel columns, beams, girders, slabs, and other structural parts, also sizes and position of all floor openings.

The drawings are to show the area and location of all steel reinforcing members to be placed in all parts of the work.

There must be likewise submitted schedule showing the manner in which it is proposed to bond the steel rods for all parts and the spacing of stirrups and their size and design. These drawings shall be submitted as soon as possible after closing of the contract and no form work shall be done until after the approval of these drawings.

The approval of drawings does not in any way relieve the contractor of his responsibility for the safety of the design.

LOADS

The loads for which the reinforced concrete has been designed are indicated on plans and are in addition to dead load composed of all construction, whether concrete, wood, or otherwise.

STRESSES

In computing sizes of members the following stresses are to be used:
Steel in tension	20,000# per sq. in.
Concrete in Extreme Fibre	750# per sq. in.
Concrete in direct compression	560# per sq. in.
Concrete in shear	40# per sq. in.
Soil bearing approximately	2,700# per sq. ft.

SAND

The sand whall be clean, washed coarse bank sand, gravel or coarse river gravel, free from dirt or other impurities. Sand shall contain less than two percent (2%) of loam. Sand shall be submitted to architect for approval and all sand shall be equal to approved sample.

STONE

The broken stone shall consist of clean, hard rock, as approved by the Architect, or Owner's Superintendent. The stone used for other concrete in large mass may be of a size to pass the a 2" ring, and one-fourth($\frac{1}{4}$) of the whole shall be less than $\frac{1}{2}$ of the maximum size.

Stone for floors shall be broken to pass a 3/4" ring. All stone shall be free from crusher dust.

Gravel shall be clean, free from loam or organic matter and shall be of such aggregate that when screened on $\frac{1}{4}$" mesh screen, 70% by volume or 60% by weight shall be held on the screen, and not more than 30% by volume or 40% by weight shall pass through, and of the material passing through not more than 30% shall pass through a #40 mesh.

Care shall be exercised to keep the gravel or sand and broken stone in distinct and separate bins and piles.

CEMENT

All cement used shall be American Portland, of approved manufacture, and subject to the tests as hereinafter specified.

PROPORTION

All concrete for floors and beams shall be mixed in proportions of one part cement, two parts sand, and four parts broken stone 1:2:4.

All concrete for columns shall be mixed in proportions of one part cement, one and one-half parts sand, and three parts stone, 1:1-1/2:3.

All concrete for footings and foundation walls shall be mixed in proportions of one part cement, three parts sand, and four parts stone, 1:3:4.

When sand and aggregate are combined in gravel as previously specified, the following substitutions will be considered equivalent to the above proportions:

1:2:4 mixture equals one Portland Cement 4-1/2 gravel

1:1-1/2:3 mixture equals one Portland Cement 3-1/4 gravel

1:3:4 mixture equals one Portland Cement 5 gravel

SHIPMENTS

All shipments are to consist of fresh cement, to meet the following specific specifications:

All cement shall be purchased subject to the standard costs of the American Society for Testing Materials, as most recently adopted with all subsequent amendments. These tests shall be made in strict accordance with the methods prescribed by the Committee on Uniform Tests of the American Society of Civil Engineers.

Before any change is made to comply with the local ordinances or laws, the contractor shall notify the Architect in writing of required change, and have his written approval of said change.

Cement shall be delivered in suitable bags with brand name of manu-facturer plainly marked thereon.

STORAGE

At least twelve days' time is to be allowed for inspection and necessary tests before using.

IN order to allow ample time for inspection and testing, cement should be stored in large quantities in suitable weather-tight building on the premises, having floor properly blocked or raised from the ground. The cement shall be stored in such manner as to permit easy acces for proper inspection and identification of each shipment or carload.

TESTS OF CEMENT

Cement tests to be made by same laboratory approved by the Architect and paid for by the contractor.

Reports of test shall go to the architect and contractor simultaneously.

Cement samples to be tested must be representative of the let or ship-metn, i.e., samples must be made up of parts selected at random from all parts of the single let or shipment.

Contractor to have cement on promises at least two weeks previous to using, so as to cause no delay in the event of cement not testing up to standards.

Cement failing to meet seven day requirements must be held awaitng results of twenty-eight day requirements.

All tests shall be made in accordance with methods accepted by American Society for Testing Material, together with all amendments thereto. Any cement which has air set shall not be used.

FALSE FORM, FORMS, CENTERING & SHORES

The Contractor shall perform all labor and furnish all material for the construction of all forms and woodwork necessary to complete the concrete work. The forms are to be so constructed that they can be taken down without damaging the concrete or spalling the corners.

All forms shall be made true to line, plumb and level. The contractor shall provide bevelled strips in the bottom angles of all beam and girder forms where directed, and lever the centering to form ceiling angles, perfectly true.

The method of centering is to permit of the earlier removal of the slab forms and sides of beams and the leaving in position of the shores and bottom forms of beams and girders.

A sufficient number of shores for the proper support of the forms, the dead weights of the wet concrete and the loads incidental to place, shall be provided, and shall rest on a solid foundation and remain in position until the concrete is sufficiently strong to support the weight of any upper floors which may depend upon such shores.

Care shall be exercised to see that the soil where used is suitable for the support of the bottom struts, and does no compress under the load. If the latter conditions prevail, trussed supports shall be provided for the forms.

Forms shall be sufficiently rigid to avoid any deflection whatever.

All forms for the entire work shall be made with smooth dressed material accurately put together and neatly filled. No marred or twisted boards shall be used in the construction of the face of the molds, and all molds are to be thoroughly swept and cleaned before the concrete is laid.

Any necessary form work shall be provided, also for making openings where required for the installation of the equipment.

All forms shall be wahed off with water from a hose or by other means, sometime before and again immediately before the concrete is poured, or order to swell the wood to a tight fit and to remove any foreign substance.

In using water on forms care shall be exercised so that water shall not gather at bottom of forms or on wet concrete.

In dry weather hollow tile floors shall be wet before the pouring of concrete.

REMOVING OF FORMS

No forms shall be removed without the consent of the superintendent.

Forms shall be removed carefully in order to avoid scarring or spalling the concrete, and to prevent heavy forms from falling on and jarring the floors.

The concrete shall be sounded frequently with a hammer during the removal of the forms to make sure that the concrete is sound and well set.

The sides of girder and beam frames shall not be removed within six (6) days after pouring, except in case where such forms do not carry any vertical load, when they may be removed in forty-eight (48) hours after pouring.

The minimum time which shall elapse before removing the shores under

the girders and beams will vary with the design and the condition of the weather,
but in no case shall the time be less than fifteen (15) days after pouring
between April 1st and November 15th, and in no case less than twenty-five
(25) days after pouring between November 15th and April 1st.

The minimum time which shall elapse after pouring before removing the
shores under floor slabs shall be ten (10) days between April 1st and November
15th, and twenty (20) days between November 15th and April 1st.

During the period between November 15th and April 1st permission may
be obtained in writing from the Architect to remove forms in less time than
stated above; provided, that in the opinion of the Architect, proper precaustions
are being taken, and that responsibility for accidents is assumed by the
contractor. In no case, however, shall forms under beams and girders be
removed in less than fifteen (15) days, nor those under slabs within ten (10)
days during the period stated above.

The times given above are minimum times in all cases, and in no case
shall shores be removed before the concrete is set hard and has sufficient
strength to safely carry its own weight and all additional loads bearing upon
it or about to be put upon it.

The builder orhis representative in charge of concrete construction shall
always be present during the removal of forms and shall be personally responsible for the safety of this operation at all times and under all conditions.
During the winter months, no shores shall be removed until portions of the
concrete have been chipped off and removed to a warm place and tested for
frost or ice.

STORING OF STEEL ON THE JOB
Steel when arriving at the job shall be stored in rain-proof shelter,
kept clear of the ground and shall be placed in some tabulated order, so that
any particular piece can be readily located.

None of the steel reinforcement shall be badly rusted, although a thin
film of rust is not be considered objectionable. If a badly rusted new bars
shall be obtained and rusted ones removed from premises. If the steel is
covered with loose or scaly rust, dirt or cement drippings, it shall be cleaned
with a wire brush. All bars shall be free from grease or paint.

PLACING REINFORCEMENT
All steel shall be set in proper position in the molds before the concrete
is poured and the reinforcement shall be solidly supported or hung therein in
such a manner as to prevent shifting about when the concrete is tamped,
care being taken to maintain the bars in their proper position.

All steel shall be properly wired together where required using an
annealed wire of suitable size.

All reinforcing steel shall have a protection of concrete not less than
one and one-half ($1\frac{1}{2}$) inches thick for reinforced columns, one and one-half
($1\frac{1}{2}$) inches thick on the bottom and side of girders and beams, and three-
quarters (3/4) inch on the bottom of the floor slabs.

PIPE SLEEVES
The Contractor shall place sleeves on the slab centering in order to
provide holes for the use of plumbing steam, electrical conduits, etc. where they
pass through slabs. Said sleeves being furnished by the contractors for the

respective kinds of work and drawings, also being furnished by the contractor,
showing the proper location of said sleeves.

MIXING

It is the intention of these specifications to obtain a heavy dense concrete,
and sample mixes shall be made to accurately determine the proper proportions.
These mixes shall be tested by both weight and volume. All subject to the
City Rules of the Local Building Code. Suitable means shall be provided, as
approved by the Architect, for accurately measuring the respective ingredients.

An approved Batch Mixer such as the Ransome, McKelvey, Smith or
Chicago types and of sufficient capacity shall be used. Continuous mixer
machine shall not be allowed to be used. Mixing shall be thorough, and each
batch shall be left at least one minute in the mixer after the addition of the
last water.

A competent man shall be in charge of the mixing. Care shall be
exercised in adding water to obtain the proper consistency. Water should be
added by measure, not by hose, in order to avoid non-uniformity, and in
such quantity as to make a concrete of jelly-like consistency which shall
quake in the forms but on which free water shall not appear unless trowelled
or patted.

HAND MIX

Where the quantity of work is small, hand mixing may be permitted
by the Architect, in which case the cement and sand shall be turned over with
shovels, twice while dry and twice while being wet.

The water shall be added in such a manner as not to wash out the
cement. The stone shall be wet separately before being added and the whole
turned over together twice with shovels. Concrete of even color must be
obtained and concrete must be mixed on a proper mixing board.

CONTRACTOR'S PLANT

The contractor shall provide a suitable hoist and all other tools and im-
plements for handling the concrete with the greatest possible dispatch.

If steam hoist is used, engine shall be kept out of building.

PUTTING CONCRETE IN PLACE

All concrete shall be distributed evenly, and shall not be dumped at
one place and worked along by means of a hoe or other tool.

No concrete shall be dumped from a greater height than 5 ft. Wherever
necessary a chute of wood or metal must be used. The concrete shall be
well tamped in position, filling all voids and making solid dense concrete,
and themolds throughout filled, with all stone worked back from forms so
that when the forms are removed the work will be smooth on the face and
solid throughout.

All concrete work when exposed shall have the rough parts smoothed
off and the voids filled with mortar of cement and sand in same proportion
as specified for concrete leaving a smooth finish.

All columns, girders and beams shall be plumb, straight and true to a
line, special care being exercised in these particular with the columns and wall
forms.

Slabs and beams shall be poured in one continuous operation and where

the work of one day joins that of the next the junction shall be made in
the following manner: As soon as the work has stopped for the day, the upper
portion of all fresh concrete shall be removed with a trowel to the full
depth of the laitance, and in all cases to a depth of at least 3/4".

Before starting to pour, the areas of contact shall be well cleaned with
water well soaked so that old cement will take up no more moisture, and then
grouted with neat cement rubbed in with brushes or brooms, thereafter a
thin layer of cement mortar shall be trowelled in and slabs immediately laid.
The same applies to the beams.

STOPPING WORK

If concreting must be stopped before an entire floor is completed, the
stop shall be made in center of beams and center of floor slabs.

The place where concrete work is stopped must be at right angles to
direction of beams or slabs. In no event shall work be terminated in beams
or floor slabs, where future shearing action becomes great, as at the beam
ends, or directly under a heavily concentrated load. The beams and slabs shall
be poured in one continuous operation and under no circumstances should the
lower portion of beam be poured up to the bottom of slab without continuing
the work on the entire beam.

CAUTION

After the floor slabs have begun to set, they are NOT TO BE WALKED
ON OR WHEELED OVER UNTIL HARD, as otherwise their strength is
seriously injured. If traffic over them is unavoidable planks shall be provided
for the purpose of distributing the weights.

LAYING CONCRETE IN COLD WEATHER

Reinforced concrete should not be laid, if it is possible to avoid doing
so, when the temperature is below 26 degrees Fahr.. Extra precautions shall
be taken during cold weather. The water shall be heated to about 100 degrees
Fahr. The stone and san,d if covered with ice or snow, should be heated by
steam immediately before mixing.

Should the temperature drop below freezing or the weather bureau
predict such weather, fresh concrete is to be protected by a thick layer
of hay or straw above it, and salamander fires or other heat provided below.
The openings shall be covered where necessary.

A quantity of hay or straw should be kept on hand, for use in covering
the work.

Concrete frozen while fresh and found to be injured shall be removed
at the Contractor's expense.

Forms shall be left in place furing cold weather until the concrete
has obtained a hard natural set. Under no circumstances shall salt be used
in the concrete.

TESTS OF CONCRETE

If the strength of any part of the building should be questioned by the
Architect, due to faulty material, poor workmanship or inaccuracy on pary
of contractor, the contractor at the end of one month, after removal of forms,
test the part in question. It is to stand a load equal to twice the live load,
for which it was designed. With this load there shall not be a deflection

exceeding 1/400 part of the span and floor should return to normal position
after load is removed.

The expense of such tests to be borne entirely by the contractor.

One test as before mentioned shall be placed on slab selected by the
Architect, or the superintendent, on each floor and roof, before acceptance
of building.

FIREPROOFING STEEL

All exposed steel shall be fireproofed by this contractor except roof
trusses and roof beams, and including all existing steel beams showing exposed
surfaces.

Beams shall be wrapped separately with not less than No. 12 wire and
poured solid with concrete, care being taken to keep forms 2" clear of steel
to ensure a complete and homogeneous covering of concrete not less than 2"
thick on all steel surfaces.

Columns may be treated in similar fashion, or may be fireproofed
with brick or hard burned clay tile laid up in cement mortar.

<u>GENERAL</u>

It is the intention of these specifications to include allthat is considered best in theory and practice. Special attention must be given in this construction to quality of labor, material and character of workmanship.

All work herein specified must be executed strictly in accordance with good building regulations. These specifications and all requirements for good structure must be met by the contractor, whether covered by plans and specifications or not.

The contracter on this work is to co-operate with all other contractors in the securing of properly constructed building. He is to notify the plumber and heating contractor at proper time to obtain sleeves and the location of same for passage of pipes.

Notify proper contractor so as to obtain anchors for suspended ceiling, pipe hangers, etc. so that same can be placed in forms at proper time, placing Bond Anchors and beams for anchoring of brickwork, etc. In a general way he is to see that all work coming in contact with reinforced concrete is properly provided for without future cutting and alteration.

BRICKWORK

All common brickwork shall be laid up true and plumb with a shove joint in full bed of cement mortar, all joints carefully filled.

Brickwork shall be laid up to a line on both sides in common bond of stretchers, every sixth course being a full header course, joints truly horizontal and vertical, bond being correctly maintained with vertical joints in line, horizontal and vertical joints of uniform width, and shall be finished with struck joints on exposed surfaces unless otherwise specified, including all unplastered portions of basement.

COMMON BRICK

Common brick shall be hard and well burned, true to shape and uniform in quality and size and shall be used wherever indicated by diagonal hatching on the plans.

Wherever brick, tile or salvaged stone work is used as a backing against present or new construction, care must be taken to form an ample bond between new and old work. Proper anchors shall be provided and secured to present masonry where necessary to make a proper and acceptable job and as approved by the Architect or superintendent.

TERRA COTTA TILE

Terra Cotta tile as herein specified may be used in such portions of the work as approved by the Clerk of Works or Architect. This applies to new and rebuilt portions of present building.

All walls above grade level, interior 8" thick and over, may be built of Denison Interlocking Tile in cement mortar, unless otherwise specified. They shall be faced with stone on exterior as indicated on the drawings or as specified. Special tile shall be used for all jambs and corners and for bond in 16" walls. All piers, however, 2 feet or less in width shall be built of brick only.

PLUMBING & LEVELLING OF DOOR FRAMES

This contractor shall be responsible for the keeping plumb and level of all door and window frames, after having been set by other contractors.

SETTING OF IRON WORK

Set in correct position and build in all anchors for iron ladders, and architectural iron work in general, set all manhole, pipe trench and trap pit covers, and bed all template for structural steel.

SETTING OF IRON WINDOW FRAMES

This contractor shall set and properly anchor to the present stone all iron frames. They shall be secured to the satisfaction of the Architect or his Superintendent. If any special drilling or cutting is necessary, he shall do same or arrange with stone mason to do this work for him, paying for the cost of such work.

SPECIAL FOUNDATION

Heating contractor shall build concrete or brick foundations for fans and motors, following sizes and dimensions on heating plans and details, and using concrete in proportions $1\frac{1}{2}$ to 3.

ARCHES

Build brick relieving arches to take the weight of the lintels over doors and windows and brick ledges for the support of all reinforced concrete, etc. as required by the drawings.

All brick arches in face brick shall be carefully and truly built exactly conforming to drawings and details. Carpenter shall provide centering, this contractor shall set and maintain same and shall be responsible for its removal.

Centering shall not be removed until permission of the Architect is obtained.

CHASES

The Mason Contractor shall examine the wiring, heating, plumbing and construction drawings and shall leave all chases required by and for same, and shall work under the instructions of the various contractors for the above items, and perform all work so as to avoid cutting as much as possible.

CUTTINGS

The Mason shall do all cutting of masonry, brickwork or stonework required by any of the other contractors employed on the job, and after their work has been installed he shall patch up around same in neat and tradesmanlike fashion.

He shall also do the necessary cutting for the bearing of beams carrying the floor loads at wall. This cutting must be done so as to give a uniform true and well bearing to all beams.

All chases, however, not more than 2" x 2" or requiring less than 8 hours continuous labor, shall be made and repaired by the contractor requiring them.

FILLING HOLES IN MASONRY

When floor beams are all set, all holes and openings around same are to be cemented in tight, also any holes in the present masonry that are unnecessary or may have resulted from the fire. This applies not only to the floor sections but to the entire present building.

ANCHORS & WALL TIES

Wherever stonework is built against concrete or other masonry "Security" anchor strips shall be placed in the forms in such fashion that there shall be two strips vertically, one on each side of each corner of all columns, and at least two strips on face of all columns, and on other portions of the masonry at such spacings as will give an average of one wall tie to every square foot of mason work. The mason work shall be bonded to these wall ties by means of "Security" anchors set by the mason as the wall is built.

CLEANING & POINTING

All new stone work shall be thoroughly cleaned on completion. Point up close to all sills, casings, projections, and leave the whole work in perfect condition.

At completion of the job, sand blast the entire face stone work on both new and old work and give a uniformly clean finished exterior.

DWARF WALLS

Build all dwarf walls or small retaining walls necessary to receive beams, sills, partitions, or at changes in basement level, as shown on drawings.

WALL COVERING

Provide all needful materials with which to cover the walls from action of the weather at all times.

DAMP COURSE

On foundations at grade line, below first course of stone, place a damp course of 3 ply "Barrett or equal" ready roofing extending through the wall, and neatly cut off flush with face of wall.

SCOPE OF WORK

The kitchen, community room of basement, stairs No. 2 & 3, also all toilets and lavatories throughout are to be of Gibraltar Floors surface with bases of same material 6" in height which are to finish with rounded top $\frac{1}{4}$" beyond face of wall above.

CEMENT FLOOR BY MASON

The Mason Contractor will level and tamp thoroughly excavated portions of basement, overlay with 4" of broken stone or clean coal cinders, thoroughly tamped and solidified. Thereafter lay on a 4" concrete covering in proportions of 1:2:4 and leave ready to receive a Gibraltar Floor. Finish floor as specified.

GIBRALTAR FLOORS

Screens for this floor to be set at $\frac{1}{4}$" of top finished level, after slab is partially set. This Gibraltar floor will consist of a plastic mix of one part cement and two parts of Granite Chips which are to be packed and rolled to a dense surface. After floor has been properly set depending on weather conditions it is to be ground to a level, dustless finish which is to show not less than 60% of Granite Chips on surface. Before completion it is to be given a final light grinding and washing and left in a perfect condition. General color to be a light tone.

The Mason contractor to make provision for cement bases where elsewhere specified.

CONCRETE FLOORS & STEPS

Where indicated on drawings build concrete floor and steps in proportion as heretofore specified.

TERRAZZO

Floors of crypt and crypt vestibule and Stair No. 1 or elsewhere so indicated shall be surfaced with terrazzo consisting of marble chips and Portland Cement mixed to the consistency of stiff paste, spread to an average thickness of 5/8" and ground perfectly smooth and level, free of all humps, hollows or irregularities, and showing on surface not less than 85% marble.

All terrazzo floors shall have a border strips 6" wide and cove bases 6" high with $1\frac{1}{2}$" radius coves. Bases against tile partitions shall be reinforced with an approved manufacture of metal lath.

The treads of stairs No. 1 will be of terrazzo.

Border strip shall be divided from field, and field shall be divided into sections as directed, with lines. Brass strips as indicated by final detailed drawings.

Field of floors in General shall be white marble with about 10% of
colored marble added, base and border shall have 50% of colored marble.
Treads of stairs shall have 20% of alundum chips. On completion all
terrazzo shall be cleaned, protected with sawdust till completion of job, and
then again cleaned and handed over in perfect condition.

CEMENT FINISH

All floor areas marked or specified for cement or linoleum or rubber
tile shall be finished with topping 1" thick as above specified. Before topping
is applied the surface of the slab shall be thoroughly flushed with clean water
and thereafter treated with bonding liquid manufactured by the Bradford
Chemical Co., Detroit, applied according to the directions of the manufacturers.
WHERE SPEARATE FIGURE IS REQUIRED OR FOR WOOD FLOORS
INDICATED THE FOLLOWING SHALL GOVERN:

CINDER FILL

Fill between sleepers of all new wood floors with mix consisting of one
part cement, two parts sand and seven parts clean soft coal cinders, well
tamped and finished with $\frac{1}{4}$" thickness of cement martar screeded level with
top of sleepers.

TILE PARTITIONS & BACKING

All partitions and wall furring shown on drawings cross hatched, except
fireproofing of steel columns, or elsewhere so marked are to be hard burned
clay tile and shall be of gypsum block of Acme, American, or U.S. Gypsum
Co. manufacture, laid up in mortar consisting of one part gypsum to three
parts sand.
All partitions shall be erected perfectly plumb and true of thickness
as shown with broken joints, and shall be built secure and rigid well wedged
up under slab at ceilings.
All openings over 4 feet wide not otherwise shown or specified shall
have self supporting flat arches formed in partition blocks and reinforced
with $\frac{1}{4}$" flat bar reinforcement over same, supplied and installed by this
contractor.

WOOD SLEEPERS FOR WOOD FLOORS

Where wood floors are specified over concrete the Mason shall build in
all bevelled sleepers which are to be furnished by Carpenter Contractor.

MASONRY ADDENDA

CONTRACTOR'S RESPONSIBILITY

REGARDING FLOORS

Before any rough floors are laid the General Contractor shall determine
from the drawings and specifications the types of floors in various parts of
the building and on each floor and make allowance where necessary for lowering
or offsetting the unfinished floors sufficient for the finished floors in all
cases to be level and even at intersections with others adjoining.

MAIN FLOORS OF CHURCH

The main floor of church is to be a cement top finish laid perfectly level and true to receive linoleum. All aisles and spaces marked for tile and marble are to be kept at least 2" below the main finished floor line for the laying of tile. Edges in all cases are to be protected and maintained perfectly true and even to receive linoleum under spaces where seating is shown.

CONCRETE LINTELS

Where wood lintels are now built over basement windows, they sahll be removed and new concrete lintels built around reinforcing steel which is to have a wall bearing. These to be constructed to satisfaction of Architect's Superintendent.

FLOOR SUMPS

In 2 top floor of each tower, build in iron sumps as furnished by Roofers and make water tight. These sumps to have outlet to extend through concrete from which roofer will extend conductors.

This contractor to do the necessary cutting for one opening on side of each tower through which the conductors will extend. Cement the openings tight at completion of work.

SIDEWALKS

At the completion of the work this contractor shall repair all sidewalks both on the outside and within the grounds and leave same in perfect condition. Where sections of new walks are necessary on street, they shall be laid in accordance with the requirements of local departments having charge of public works. This work must be done to the satisfaction of the Architect or his representative.

SODDING

At completion of the job all sod within the premises that has been damaged shall be replaced with a good No. 1 Sod to conform to that now on vacant space. This will include sodding between church and both houses and between church and walks on street, side and between walks and curb.

ARCHITECTUAL TERRA COTTA

HOLY WATER BASINS

Provide Holy Water basins of terra cotta in color as hereafter selected. These basins to be provided with a glass bowl which will be selected by the T. C. Co. executing this work.

This bowl which will be approximately 6" in diameter and not less than 4" deep will set into the Terra Cotta which is to be modelled to receive same. This Company will furnish 2 glass bowls for each basin required.

TOWER DOMES

The domes of each tower where marked on plans are to be of structural T. C. color and face texture as hereafter approved by Architect. The Three modelled bands are to be in contrasting colors as selected and approved.

This terra cotta to be erected and anchored in accordance with shop drawings which are to be furnished by the T. C. Co. supplying same and in accordance with the supplemental specifications of the manufacturer.

AREA WALLS

All area walls are to be rebuilt and finished with concrete coping making provision for anchorage of iron railings. The bottom of all areas to have concrete floor with bell traps connected to drain.

TOWER DOMES (Cont'd)

Also 24 perforated panels in between columns in top of present towers as shown.

Twenty four (24) panels in rail of same towers as shown.
Twelve (12) panels in rail of tower of chapel as shown including drum rail.
This includes 8 statues on main Towers.
Note: (36 panels were shown as stone.)

USABLE STONE ON PREMISES

Each contractor estimating this work shall visit the job and inspect the brown stone available on the premises.

If the available stone on hand is by his estimate insufficient to properly complete the exterior he shall state in his bid the amount of additional stone required.

REBUILT PORTIONS OF STONE WORK

Upper portions of towers with misc. portions to be rebuilt where indicated on elevations. George Powrie & Sons, Stone Masons, Marquette, Michigan, can furnish quotations on this part of work if desired.

SETTING OF IRON WORK

The Mason shall set and build in anchors for all iron ladders, set all manhole covers, pipe trench covers, etc.

He shall bed all templates for structural steel.
Steel contractor shall give proper location and levels.
Foundations for columns shall be finished at a point $\frac{1}{2}$" below true level, and Steel Contractor shall set bases to exact level position. Immediately thereafter this contractor shall grout in all the bases.

The Mason Contractor shall set all angles and loose lintels and beams of every description, all other steel work shall be set and erected by Steel Contractor.

CUT STONE WORK

Labor only for all stone work will be done under a separate contract and will not be included under the general contract. The stone mason will provide his own tools and derricks only but no permanent scaffolding.

The General Contractor will provide all scaffolding that is necessary for the entire structure and will give full use of same to the Stone Mason for the full and expeditious execution of his work. He shall build this scaffolding as and where necessary for the work as it progresses and in advance of its requirements.

The General Contractor will also be responsible for the providing of all anchors of every description to properly anchor the stone and the masonry to the stone work and shall work in connection with the Stone Masons in backing up all stone work as it progresses giving full assistance and cooperation to the Stone Contractor to avoid all delays. He shall also provide any necessary Mortar, Mortar colors, cement, structural beams, lintels foundations and wall necessary to support all stone and the cost of the stone carving and the models for same.

The same cooperation will be required of the stone contractor toward the general contractor in order that this does not unnecessarily delay the progress of the work of the general contractor. It is the intent of these specifications to promote the cooperation of both parties toward the proper execution of the work involved under their respective contracts.

All brown stone will be furnished and delivered on the site by the Owner.

The General Contractor shall cooperate with the stone contractor for its being conveniently placed when delivered and properly protected until being built into the building.

OWNER'S RESPONSIBILITY

The Owner's responsibility will cease on delivery of this material.

DELIVERY & STORAGE OF CUT STONE

This contractor shall take delivery of, cart to job, store and set all cut stone shown on drawings and as specified. All stone shall be stored at the building on a wooden platform and properly protected, and this contractor shall be responsible for its condition on reaching the job. No spalled or patched stone will be accepted or used on the job. This refers to stone other than brown stone.

ANCHORS & DOWELS

General Contractor to supply and the Stone Mason to set all anchors and dowels of heavily wrought galvanized iron as indicated on setting diagrams and wherever necessary.

Anchors shall be placed so that each stone shall have at least one anchor, and all stones two feet or over shall have one anchor for every two feet in length, and not fewer than two anchors.

SETTING MORTAR

General Contractor to supply all mortar used. Shall be lime mortar gauged with ten percent of approved non-staining cement as previously specified.

Special care shall be taken to keep stone faces clean from mortar splashes.

Any mortar falling on face of stone shall be immediately sponged off with clean water.

SETTING OF STONE

All stone shall be set in accordance with drawings and diagrams.

It shall be thoroughly sponged on all joints before setting.

Mortar shall be kept back 3/4" from face of stone to allow for pointing.

All beds and vertical joints shall be not less than 3/16" or more than $\frac{1}{4}$" in width.

Stone shall be set accurately, true to a line and level by competent stone setters.

Face stone shall be set on thoroughly wetted wooden wedges, which are not to be removed until building is cleaned and pointed.

All stone over 80 lbs. in weight shall be set with a hand derrick.

All stone shall be settled with a mallet, and any stone not coming to proper bed shall be taken up and reset.

The backs of all stone shall be thoroughly sponged with clean water and thereafter plastered with $\frac{1}{2}$" coat of setting mortar.

PAINTING OF STONE

It is expressly forbidden to paint the back of the stone with R.I.W. or any other damp-resistant paints.

BACKING

All cut stone shall be backed up with brick or tile as soon as it is set, and the backing adjacent to the stone shall be laid up in non-staining mortar.

POINTING & JOINTING

The entire face of new and old work is to be carefully pointed at completion by the Stone Mason. Mortar to be furnished by the General Contractor and colored to match present work.

The joints of all the old stone work are to be very carefully raked out wherever there is lack of complete firmness and to be properly pointed whith colored mortar as above specified.

At completion of the work and when exterior is entirely completed, sand blast all brown stone construction as specified on page 24.

CLEANING & POINTING

At completion of the job the entire stone exterior of building except new lime and sand stone shall be sand blasted to uniform the entire old and rebuilt work.

All new lime and sand stone except steps shall be cleaned with water and brush and fine sand where necessary to produce a clean finished job.

SETTING OF INSERTS

The Mason shall set all marble and tile inserts for walls supplied by Contractor for that work.

MAIN WINDOW

The stone work of main window shall be as detailed of Ohio Sandstone.

All work requiring carving on these windows shall be executed at the yard of the company furnishing the material. Models for this work are to be secured from the Parducci Studios, 1241-10th St., Detroit, MI. Cost of same including shipment to be paid for by the company furnishing the stone. All stone carving is to be clean cut and executed in strict accordance with details and models furnished.

INTERIOR WAINSCOTING

All wainscoting indicated stone shall be of Coughlin Quarry Cream Mankato Stone. It shall be $1\frac{1}{4}$" in thickness, set true and plumb and be securely anchored to furring. This material is to be stricktly within ranger of color of two samples which are to be furnished to the Architects and all stone not conforming to sample range will be rejected.

This Contractor shall cut all wainscoting as may be necessary to fit to heating grilles, registers or other necessary requirements of the drawings, if wainscoting is included.

This contractor may give a separate estimate on wainscoting of other similar stone, the requirements of which shall be as specified under the preceding paragraph.

CUTTING

All exposed faces shall be cut true, full to the square, with joints as required, arrises full and true, beds, ends, and tops dressed straight and at right angles to the face unless otherwise shown. There washes are not indicated on

the details they shall be made as steep as practical, and drips shall be provided
of sufficient depth to shed water on all projecting stone and courses.

FINISH

The finish on all exposed surfaces shall be smooth unless otherwise
specified.

SHOP DRAWINGS

Complete Cutting and Setting drawings based upon the Architect's drawings
and details, shall be prepared by the Contractor in triplicate and submitted for
the Architect's approval. They shall show in detail sizes and dimensions,
arrangement of joints and bonding, anchoring and other necessary details.

Each stone indicated on these drawings shall bear the corresponding
number.

PATCHING

No spalled or patched stone is to be used.

CARTAGE & SHIPPING

All cut stone shall be shipped and carted, properly protected by means
of wood angle covers and excelsior.

CARVING & LETTERING

All carving shall be executed by an approved carver from models approved
by the Architects and lettering shall be in strict accordance with full size details.

MODELS

This Contractor shall supply all models required for carving. Models must
be approved by the Architect before any stone cutting is done. All models to
be furnished by Parducci Studios, who will furnish quotations on same.

CORNER STONE OF CHAPEL

This stone shall be panelled on two exposed sides with inscription all
as detailed. Provide space for sheet metal box 5" x 5" x 10" cut out of the
solid stone and face of stone to be as detailed.

STRUCTURAL IRON & STEEL WORK

**THE GENERAL CONDITIONS AND GENERAL CONTRACTOR'S SPEC-
IFICATIONS IN THE FRONT OF THESE SPECIFICATIONS TOGETHER WITH
THE FOLLOWING TO GOVERN THIS WORK.**

GENERAL

This specification is intended to include the supply and erection of all
Structural Iron Work shown on the drawings and required by the nature of the
job unless specified under another heading.

All structural iron shall be the best of its kind, as regards to quality
of material and workmanship and shall strictly comply with plans as regards to
dimensions.

This specification is intended to provide for complete work including
all necessary connections and details requisite for erection, and to develop the
full strength of the structure. Such details are to be considered as specified,
and are to be provided by the contractor without additional charge.

Apparent discrepancies in plans or specifications must be referred to
the Architect, whose decision shall be final, and work done without such decision
shall be at the contractor's risk.

Beams and lintels of every description will be included under the Structural
Iron Contract.

The Architects reserve the right to reject any and all materials or work
at any time before the completion of the building, if in his judgment either
do not comply with the terms of these specifications and good practice, andh
his decision as to the true intent of plans and specifications shall be final.

DELIVERIES

Deliveries shall be made in the order required for construction and at
the time specified in the contract.

WEIGHTS

Any individual member or piece of material which weighs less than
the proper weight may be condemned at the discretion of the Architect.

STEEL

All materials shall be new stock. No salvaged or reworked material is
to be used. Weights and dimensions of all wide flange beams and American
standard beams and channels to be in accordance with the practice adopted by
the Association of American Steel Manufacturers. Quality of material and
workmanship shall strictly comply with Architects' drawings.

All steel shall be of "Open Hearth Process" and shall conform to the
current standard specifications for "Structural Sttel for Building" of the American
Society for Testing Materials.

In all cases this contractor must furnish the exact sections weights and
kinds of material called for an Architects drawings and he must follow the
exact details, methods and instructions call for by this specifications and
drawings to their true intent and purpose. The substitution of different shapes
for those specified will be permitted when conditions of supplying equal strength

are met, and when no interference with architectural or other features of the
work is caused by the change.

All workmanship shall correspond to the requirements of "The American
Institute of Steel Construction" in their Standard Specifications dated June 1, 1923.

<u>DRAWINGS</u>

All working shop plans shall conform to the plans furnished by the
Architect, and must bear their signature of approval before work commences.
Such approval, however, shall not relieve the shop from the responsibility of
correcting without charge, any errors in not following the Architect's plans,
or errors of "clearance" or "connections" which can be discovered by examination.

At least two sets of working plans and two copies of order lists of
material shall be furnished to the Architect.

<u>PUNCHING</u>

All rivet holes shall be accurately spaced in a true line, and laid out
by template. The clearance between die and punch shall not exceed 1/32"
for material ½" thick, nor 3/64" for thicker material. Holes shall be clean-
cut without cracks, and burrs shall be removed by a counter-sinking reamer.

<u>STRAIGHTENING</u>

The material for all build members shall be straightened after punching.

<u>ASSEMBLING</u>

At assembling, and before riveting, built members shall be truly straight,
and out of "wind" held by a sufficient number of bolts to prevent warping or
bending under handling and riveting. No drifting or holes shall be done under
any circumstances in any class of work, but failure of holes to match shall
be corrected by new material or by remaining at the discretion of the Architect
or their representative.

<u>RIVETS</u>

Rivets shall be of soft steel driven by machine wherever practicable.
They shall completley fill the holes and be tight with neat cup-shaped heads
concentric with the holes and free from cracks at edges. Rivets showing
evidence of burning will be rigidly condemned. In removing defective rivet
any injury to the material will be cause of condemnation of injured parts.

Rivets shall be used for all shop work and for field work where practicable
where bolts are used in the field care shall be taken to have all bolts in a
joint in bearing at the same time, and the bolted joint shall be made at least
twenty percent stronger than the riveted joint.

<u>CONNECTIONS</u>

All joints shall be fully spliced.

Connections shall be made by rivets or tunned bolts fitting tight, as shown
on plans.

All framed beams shall be secured in position by angle brackets and
standard connections.

Any beam or girder thatis longer or more than ½" shorted than required
for its special place shall be rejected. The accurate adjustment of the lengths
of framed beams shall be made by reaming connection-holes and setting out
angle-brackets, at their ends to correct length.

BEARING PLATES

Steel or Iron Bearing Plates shall be provided under the wall ends of all beams and girders or trusses, and where not indicated on drawings shall be of such dimensions as to properly distribute the maximum load to the Masonry according to its carrying capacity.

SEPARATORS

Where two or more beams or other shapes assembled as a single supporting member they shall be securely butted together with a sufficient number of not less than 3/4" bolts thru cast iron separators or heavy wrought iron pipe to insure unity of action of the several sections.

ANCHORS

All beams resting on walls are to be securely anchored by approved T anchors built into the wall.

CHARACTER OF MATERIALS

All beams, channels, trusses, column material shall be of steel. All rivets of steel connecting angles and plates of steel. Tie rods, bolts, anchors and lateral ties of wrought iron.

COLUMNS

Columns shall be made as indicated on drawings.

This contractor shall include all labor and material required for making splices with existing columns.

In general, columns must be connected to column by splice plates on the side, riveted to the flanges of the channels with twelve (12) rivets in each column. These plates must be 3/8" thick, except where the metal of the columns connected is 3/4" thick, or more, in which case the splice plates must be ½" thick. Where the outside measurement of one column is less than the other a clearance of more than 1/16" must be taken up with fillers made of bars 3" x 1/16" punched the same as splice-plates.

All columns will have 3/4" cap-plates. All columns shall be milled at each end to a smooth bearing-surface at right angles to the columns. The contractor will be required to furnish the Architect with a drawing or schedule showing the heights at which he desires to make these cuts, showing the length of each column and the relation of each cut to the bottom of the regular floor-beams of the floor at the same level, for his approval. The number of rivets required in connections supporting beams must be calculated on a basis of the floor loads, as noted on the plans, or on the basis of the full capacity of the beam carrying an evenly distributed load, whichever may require the larger number.

BASES

Bases where required shall be built up of angles and plates all as detailed anchor bolted to concrete base installed by mason. This contractor shall provide bolts and templates and shall supervise setting of bolts and be responsible for their correct position. He shall set and level column bases and shall supervise grouting of same by mason.

TIE RODS

Tie-rods must be provided as shown on plans. These rods must be made with two nuts.

TEMPORARY BRACING
        This Contractor shall provide all necessary temporary bracing required
to support steel until construction is complete and permanently braced.

LINTELS
        This Contractor shall provide all angle iron lintels as shown and as
required for all openings in masonry walls, not shown with arches, over all
radiator recesses, etc.
        All such small loose mamebers will be set by mason.

HANGERS FOR RUNWAYS
        Provide all necessary hangers for runways as indicated on drawings and
details, all securely rivetted to the adjacent construction, and hangers and
supports for ladder over sanctuary arch.

HANGERS FOR SCAFFOLDING
        Provide and bolt to each and every truss including diagonal trusses
4" lengths of 1½" inside iam. iron pipe reaching from truss to plaster line of
ceiling, for passage of ropes for attaching decorator's scaffolding. Ends of
pipes shall be flush with plaster and shall be cut to accurately conform to
curve of ceiling.

INSPECTION
        The rolling and manufacture of iron and steel work will be inspected at
foundries, mills and shops by inspectors appointed by and responsible to the
Architect. The iron contractor shall include an amount of sixty-five (65)
cents per net tons of iron, and steel work to meet the cost of such services,
and the inspectors shall jointly represent the Architect and the contractor
at the places of manufacture, and shall report the progress of the work, and
otherwise facilitate the prompt and orderly delivery of satisfactory materials.
        The inspection, acceptance, or failure to inspect shall in no way relieve
the iron contractor or the foundries, mills or shops from their responsibility
to furnish satisfactory materials strictly in accordance with the contract,
plans and specifications.

PAINTING
        All paint shall be by the Detroit Graphite Co. or other equal approved
manufacture and each coat shall be of different color. All metal work (except
brass or plated work) shall receive one shop coat and one after erection. Any
surface inaccessible after erection shall receive two coats in the shop.
        Before any painting is done all surfaces shall be thoroughly cleaned
and left free from rust and grease. Erection marks shall be made on the
painted surface, not on the base metal then oiled over.
        After erection and before finishing coat is applied, the metal shall be
retouched and filed rivets and bots shall be painted as soon as practical after
driving. All bolts are to remain permanently in the structure shall be dipped
in the paint before being placed in position.
        No painting shall be done in wet or freezing weather and all surfaces
must be perfectly dry when paint is applied. All paint shall be applied in a
workmanlike manner, each coat evenly spread over the surface and well brushed
out, all marks of brush and laps being removed. Care shall be taken that paint

surfaces shall be coated with a mixture of white lead and tallow before being
exposed to the weather.

EXTERIOR IRON WORK

All exterior iron work shall have one coat of aluminum paint over the
graphite paint before finishing paint is applied by the painting contractor.

STEEL JOISTS

The General Conditions are a part of this specification.

All floor where so indicated, shall be supported by Truss Steel Joists
manufactured by the Truscon Steel Co., Detroit, Michigan or equal. Joists
shall be built of new billet rolled steel of structural grade, and shall conform
strictly to the manufacturers' published standards, meeting the requirements of
the specification of the American Institute of Steel Construction. All joists
shall be given one shop coat of good quality lead and oil paint.

The joist spacings shown on the drawings shall not be exceeded and joists
shall be supplied capable of safely supporting the unit live loads specified;
together with all dead loads and cross partitions. All partitions parallel with
joists to be supported on double joists.

JOIST BEARING

Where steel joists bear on masonry, a bearing of not less than four inches
shall be provided. Where supported on structural steel, a bearing of not less
than three inches is to be provided. All joists are to have a bearing end
two and one half inches deep and supporting walls and steel work shall be
finished at the proper elevation so as to afford a true and horizontal bearing.
No temporary bearings for joist support will be allowed. Necessary framing
for small openings shall be provided by the joist manufacturer and clearly shown
on his erection drawings.

JOIST BRIDGING

Steel joists shall be bridged with rigid steel bridging, as manufactured
by Truscon Steel Co. or equal and installed according to the manufacturers
specifications.

TOP LATH

The riblath used for the support of the concrete floors shall be 3/4"
riblath weighing not less than four and one half pounds per square yard, and
shall be firmly attached to the top chords of the joists through the use of
lath clips furnished by the joist manufacturer. These clips are to be used
in accordance with the manufacturers' standards so as to form a positive
connection between the joists and the concrete slab.

FLOOR FINISH

Where a terrazzo or other composition floor finish is to be laid over the
concrete slab, these finishes are to be applied strictly in accordance with specifications furnished by the manufacturers.

Steel joists other than those specified above may be used if appraised
by the Architect or his Engineer.

MISCELLANEOUS IRON WORK

<u>THE GENERAL CONDITIONS AND GENERAL CONTRACTOR'S SPEC-
IFICATION IN THE FRONT OF THESE SPECIFICATIONS TOGETHER WITH THE
FOLLOWING TO GOVERN THIS WORK.</u>

this Contractor shall provide all manner of iron and steel or metal work
mentioned in these specifications, or shown on the plans and not previously
specified under another heading.

SHOP DRAWINGS

Before any work is started or material ordered, the Contractor shall submit
in duplicated for the Architect's approval complete shop drawings showing all
details and methods of construction.

WORKMANSHIP

All work shall be neatly and carefully executed in the best fashion by
skilled tradesmen, and in strict accordance with full size details.

CASTINGS

All castings shall be of the best grey iron, clean and sharp and free
from all surface defects. All ornaments shall be cast from models approved
by the Architects. All mouldings shall be straight and true, with sharp arrises.

WROT IRON

All wrot iron shall be straight and true with sharp angles, and where bent
shall follow accurately the line of the detail. All bolt, screw, or rivet heads
shall be countersunk unless otherwise specified.

PAINTING

All paint shall be by the Detroit Graphite Co., Truscon, or other equal
approved manufacture and each coat shall be of a different color. All metal
work (except brass or plated work) shall receive one shop coat and one after
erection. Any surface inaccessible after erection shall receive two coats at
the shop.

Before any painting is done all surfaces shall be thoroughly cleaned
and left free from rust and grease. Frection marks shall be made on the
painted surface, not on the base metal then oiled over.

After erection and before finishing coat is applied, the metal shall be
retouched and field rivets and bolts shall be painted as soon as practicable
after driving. All bolts that are to remain permanently in the structure shall
be dipped in the paint before being placed in position.

No painting shall be done in wet or freezing weather and all surfaces
must be perfectly dry when paint is applied. All paint shall be applied in
a workmanlike manner, each coat evenly spread over the surface and well
brushed out, all marks of brush and laps being removed. Care shall be taken
that paint does not spread over adjacent material. All turned or planed surfaces
shall be coated with a mixture of white lead and tallow before being exposed
to the weather.

PLATED WORK

All work specified or marked for plating shall be properly prepared for
the plating tank, all surfaces perfectly smooth and clean. It shall be
finished to match samples of the adjacent hardware and shall be thoroughly
lacquered before delivery.

AREA RAILINGS

Areas on side of building shall be protected by a 1½" pipe railing as shown by drawings. Railing to have all necessary connections, elbows and base flanges to complete this work in a proper manner.

Secure railings to masonry base as approved by Superintendent to make a substantial job.

WINDOW SPANDRELS

Window Spandrels to be of 3/16" plate steel with applied Braun Molding. Sills to be of cast iron as detailed.

WINDOW GUARDS   (Separate Figure)

All windows marked W.G. to have Diamond Mesh Window Guards of 3/4" mesh of #14 wire. These guards to have a 3/8" frame with hinges secured to frame and arranged to with catch fastener on opposite side to be built in sections as approved.

RADIATOR GRILLES

All grilles for radiator enclosures, also 4 – 12 x 16 grilles and 4 – 12 x 12 Registers with louvres for Narthex, shall be furnished and installed by Iron Contractor.

The large Nave, Sanctuary and Chapel radiator grilles should have ½" x ½" mesh to prevent radiator proper from being noticeable thru mesh of grilles.

These grilles must have an angle frame to which the grille should fasten to same with countersunk brass, aluminum, or white metal countersunk stove bolts in such manner that they be easily removed. The backs and curved tops of enclosures shall have a #26 galvanized sheet metal lining well fastened to stone or brickwork of enclosrues, painted after erection with one coat of aluminum paint, before radiators are placed in recess. These metal linings to be furnished and put in place by Heating Contractor. All grilles will be of Harrington King Manufacturing Type U 66% ope., Cast Iron corners as shown by drawings.

IRON STAIRS & RAILING

Construct all steel stairs in accordance with drawings. Stringers to be of steel bent plate. Metal risers and treads to receive terrazzo finish. All as detailed.

Baluster railings of 5/8" square material not over 4" on centers. Posts square steel pipe of size as detailed. Where twisted belusters are indicated they are to be alternated plain and twisted.

ENCLOSED RADIATORS

Where so marked on plan build as detailed with stock grille facing as approved or selected.

RADIATOR SHIELDS

All radiator and air opening throughout to be provided with approved metal shields securely attached to top frame of grille facing. Type as approved by Architect.

TRAP PIT COVERS

Provide 2 - 24" trap pit covers of cast iron with a double frame as detailed. The cover to have a sub plate 3" below the top cover with Mineral Wool packed between the top and lower plate also between double frame of pit cover.

IRON LADDERS

Construct iron ladders where indicated or shown on plans of Towers.

MAIN ENTRANCE & NARTHEX DOOR FRAMES

Doors of Main entrance to Narthex and Narthex to Church shall be provided with structural channel frames with 1" x 2" stops rivetted one, having $\frac{1}{4}$" x 3" x 12" anchors, three on each side rivetted to back of frame and jambs extending at least 2" into masonry at sill and properly secured to masonry. Jambs by anchoring as approved.

This contractor shall countersink for and apply the hardware, furnished by carpenter, all securely bolted or machine screwed to the frames.

MISCELLANEOUS IRON GRILLES

Provide all wrought iron grilles where indicated and which includes gates and rails if indicated. These are all included under this contract and all to be in strict accordance with the plans and detail drawings. Sizes for metal will be as near to drawings as scale indicates. The Architect may vary shop drawings which are to be furnished by this contractor where in his judgment the sizes of metal are unsuitable to the design.

All facing (grille) shall be assembled in frames as designed. The pattern must be assembled so as not to cut into the design.

METAL CABINET DOOR

This Contractor shall furnish Mason with a metal plate cabins provided with an angle frame and angle frame with double plate door with Yale Lock or equal. This is to be built into the wall of passage. This cabinet will be approximated in depth and width as indicated on plan and 24" in height. The exact dimension however is to be furnished by Pastor. Attach strap anchors to back of cabinet to secure to masonry.

PIPE RAILINGS

Supply and install pipe railings wherever indicated by the drawings. These include area rails, handrails, side stair rails etc. Sizes as indicated by drawings or as detailed. Also see page 38.

STEEL SASH

Furnish and set all steel sash shown on plans and elevations according to standards.

Windows A-B-C-D-X-Y to be built up of sections as shown on details. Sheet #A-17.

Windows H-N-O-P-Q are Fenestra Fencraft casements or other approved type.

Windows E-F-G-I-K-J-M are Fenestra Projected Fenmark Windows rather than approved type.

All to be set with standard hardware and all windows too high are to be provided with pulls to be operated by pole. Furnish poles necessary for proper operation.

<u>SHEET METAL WORK & ROOFING</u>

<u>THE GENERAL CONDITIONS AND GENERAL CONTRACTOR'S SPECIFICATION
IN THE FRONT OF THESE SPECIFICATIONS TOGETHER WITH THE FOLLOWING
TO GOVERN THIS WORK.</u>

SOLDER

All solder shall be best grade 50% block tin. Rosin shall be used as flux and all soldered joints shall be sweated full of solder.

SHEET METAL

All sheet metal not otherwise marked or specified shall be of best grade 16 oz. copper.

WOOD MEMBERS

The Carpenter will provide all framing for attachment of tile. The carpenter will also provide the necessary bevelled battens for roof specified for copper.

METAL FLASHINGS

Metal flashings, unless otherwise specified, shall consist of flashing and counter or cap flashing. All flashings shall extend at least 6" up wall or curb. Cap flashings shall extend at least 1" into raglets or raked joints, shall be secured therein with metal wedges, shall be caulked with a mixture of Portland Cement and Barrett Co's Elastigum mixed to the consistency of a thick paste.

All joints of cap flashing shall overlap at least 3" and flashing shall have stiffening crimp along lower edge.

VALLEYS

Valleys shall be of copper open type extending at least 12" up roof on each side of valley with edges dressed over wood fillet supplied by carpenter, and shall be increased in width at lower 12 feet as indicated on drawings, to the extent of at least 15" on each side.

INSULATION

All copper shall be underlaid with 30 lb. Slaters Felt supplied and laid on the sheathing by this contractor.

TIN COVERED DOOR

Provide a metal covered door between passage leading off of upper stair landing second floor rear. This door to conform to Fire Underwriters' requirements.

METAL ROOFS

Provide all metal roofs of copper where indicated on drawings over standing battens well locked, except in valleys. Copper to be formed over these battens so as to secure a first grade roof laid in accordance with the best practice of the trade.

VENTILATORS

The Heating Contractor will supply louvres for fresh air intake, and all ventilation ducts up to roof level or as otherwise indicated.

The roofer will install ventilator connections, and shutter louvres in vent opening, chain operated.

MAIN ROOFS

Overlay all pitched surfaced marked for tile with Slaters Felt, weight not less than 30 lbs. per sq., lapping and cementing joints and tacking roofing to boarding with large headed roofing nails under the lap, carrying roofing up against all vertical walls and 4" over valley metal.

The Carpenter will supply 1" x $3\frac{1}{2}$" nailing strips, but these shall be set and nailed by the roofer at required spacing.

Tile shall be laid to straight eaves and properly locked together.

All nails shall be heavy yellow metal not less than 2" long.

All joints, at ridges or hips, shall be pointed with A.G. Horn Co's Vulcatex, colored to match tile (F.B. Stevens, Detroit Agt.)

Ridge rolls shall be nailed with $2\frac{1}{2}$" nails

All valley tile shall be angle cut.

All tile shall be the Ludovice - Celadon Co's closed shingle Red Tile line scored on face.

Samples and percentage of shades shall be submitted to and approved by the Architect before tile is ordered.

For a short space each side of valleys tile shall be laid in regular horizontal lines breaking into random laying for the balance of the surfaces.

Provide all special tile required for ridge and hip covers etc. to conform to the design.

SWEAT GUTTERS

Sweat gutters will be formed in the wood sills of large windows of front and two transepts. This contractor shall line same with 16 oz. soft copper.

CORNER STONE BOX

Provide 5" x 5" x 10" box of 16 oz. cold rolled copper with tight fitting cover, to be placed in recess of corner stone of Chapel.

GUARANTEE

Furnish to Owner written guarantee covering all roof work for a period of ten years.

LIGHTNING CONDUCTORS

Provide and install on each of the two towers Lighting Rod Conductors of $1\frac{1}{4}$" Diamete. Main Point and $\frac{1}{2}$" small point with 7 strand cable of ample capacity. The upper tip to extend through the copper finial and on inside of same and secured in such a manner as to insure proper installation at tip. Conductors to be extended to grade and properly grounded.

LOUVRES

For 2 Circular Side Gable Windows provide sheet metal G-I louvres constructed with wrought iron frame and with copper gutters secured to wall in such a manner as to prevent leakage below raggle to be cut into masonry to receive flashing. Galv. Iron to be 20-Gauge G.I. painted two (2) coats before being erected. These louvres to be so constructed as to be proof against rain and snow but to permit full ventilation. Type of louvre to be approved by Superintendent or Architect before being made. Where indicated provide copper cornice mold of 16 Oz. copper.

SNOW GUARDS

On lower parts of all roofs there shall be provided snow guards sufficient in number to insure against any snow sliding from eaves approximately 3 rows full length of roofs. These to be of Clayson type or equal as approved and secured in accordance with the manufacturer's instructions.

TOWER DRAINS

This contractor is to provide a 4" copper conductor from the 2 top floors of each tower to be arranged to drain through wall opening of tower to the roof. Supply two iron sump drains to the Mason to be built into floors of tower at low point by this contractor. The two top floors to draw on to the floor beneath.

ACOUSTONE

Base bid will be made on this material. The ceiling of Nave only will be covered with Acoustone. U.S.G. Acoustical Tile excepting the borders ribs and better circular panel which will be in other material.

This tile to be installed strictly according to the special specifications of the Manufacturer and by the Company whose material is used. The sizes, colors and pattern of ceiling to be as indicated by the drawings. Samples of tile to be furnished the Architect which will represent the extremens of shade, the final selection of color to be made before installation.

Accompanying the bid to General Contractors, this company shall furnish in duplicate one to contractor and one to Architect on accoustical analysis of reverberation based on the interior designs furnished by the drawings. The correctness of this report shall be guaranteed by the company furnishing the material selected.

As a basis of calculation, all walls are specified for Macoustic Plaster.

LATHING & PLASTERING

EXAMINATION OF WALLS

The contractor shall examine all walls, ceilings and furring he shall notify the Architect of any that are not true and securely fixed and shall see that all faults are corrected. Failure to do this, he shall, at his own expense replace in a proper manner all plastering which may have to be removed to correct such faults.

TEMPORARY HEATING

Temporary heating will be provided by the General Contractor but this contractor shall pay a share of the cost and maintenance of same. (See General Conditions).

COVERINGS

The General Contractor will enclose the building with temporary glass or cotton enclosures when directed.

PROTECTION OF WORK

The Contractor shall at all times, take proper precaution to provide against injury to the work done under this contract by the weather or from any and all causes.

Wherever necessary contractor shall protect work by means of wooden angles or frames.

SCAFFOLDING

The General Contractor will provide and erect all scaffolding required for the use of all workmen on the job.

METAL LATHING

All work specified hereunder applies to both Church and Chapel.

SCOPE OF WORK

The walls and ceilings of the entire building except such rooms as are marked unfinished shall be lathed with metal lath as herein specified. All of the ceilings of the Church and Chapel shall be suspended to meet with the requirements of the design and details. This work in its entirety shall be a part of this contract and shall be executed and erected according to the best methods and practice known to the trade. All work shall be rigidly secured by use of angles, channels and hangers as may be necessary and of sufficient sizes to insure a first class and substantial job in all respects.

METAL LATHING

Unless otherwise specified lath shall be 3 lb. Diamond Mesh Truscon or other approved brand for walls. The ceilings throughout are to be of 4 lb. weight.

It shall be secured to furring with 14 gauge annealed tieing wire, carried around furring and lath with a single turn, ends twisted tight and turned back flush with face of lath.

SUSPENDED CEILINGS

Hangers shall be $\frac{1}{4}$" round rods set 4 feet o.c. ends turned over the steel Structural members, and under the channels supporting the furring, and twisted tightly back on the rod.

SUPPORTING BARS shall be 2" Cold Rolled channels set 3 feet o.c.. Ends in all cases shall be braced tight against beams or walls, unless otherwise indicated on drawings. Where arched or dome ceilings are indicated, as in main ceiling of Church and Chapel, the curves shown on the drawings must be carefully followed and the number of hangers and braces shall be increased wherever necessary to, maintain the surface true to line.

CROSS FURRING Cross fur with 3/4" pressed steel channels 16" o.c. wired to the supporting bars with No. 14 annealed wire and leave all ready for metal lath.

WALL FURRING The outside walls above basement floor of main portion of building now standing are to be furred with 15-gauge Truscon or Youngstown Pressed Steel Box Channels, 3 ft. o.c.. This furring is to be kept in to walls as close as surface will permit. If any unusual extrusion occurs in spots it is to be brought to the attention of the General Contractor who will have same cut down to the average wall face.

When wall is made ready to receive channel furring, it is to be plugged for anchorage every 4 ft. and permanently secured to walls to the satisfaction of Architects' Superintendent. Between these channels $1\frac{1}{2}$" plasters anchoring 3/4" channels are to be placed horizontally every 16" as a stabilizer to the metal lath which on this portion of the work will be Diamond Mesh 3 lbs. weight.

WALL FURRING NEW WORK Fur all outside walls of new building and Sanctuary additions with 3/4" channels spaced $23\frac{1}{2}$" o.c.. Lath with Diamond Mesh 3 lb. weight.

Fur out wherever shown on drawings for cornices, false beams or projections and wherever required to conceal pipes or to obtain a symmetrical finish.

ADJUSTING

This contractor shall do all necessary adjusting in furring and lathing to accommodate the same to the work of other mechanics in building.

PLASTERING

All plaster materials, unless otherwise specified, shall be Acme, U.S. Gypsum Co. or American Gypsum Co. manufacture or equal approved. Plaster shall be delivered to the building in paper or cloth bags, plainly marked with the manufacturer's name and date of manufacture.

SCOPE OF WORK

See drawing for wall finish in various rooms.

SAND

All sand shall be clean, sharp, uniformly graded, containing not over 2% loam. Samples of all sand delivered to the job shall be submitted to the Architect for approval and all sand must be equal in quality to sample.

LIME

All lime shall be Ti or Brand hydrated.

IMITATION STONE MATERIAL

The following specification shall apply only in event of imitation stone being substituted for other materials.

All imitation stone plaster used on this building shall be of an approved material selected from samples furnished by the plastering contractor.

MIXING

Mortar boxes, mixing tools, etc. must be kept perfectly clean. Clean water only shall be used, and plaster is under no circumstances to be re-tampered nor shall any peices of former mix be left in the mixing box.

PROPORTIONS

Plaster shall be mixed in the following proportions:

For base coat on brick or tile 1 part plaster to 3 parts sand.

For base coat on lath 1 part plaster to 2 parts snad.

For second or brown coat, 1 part plaster to 2 parts sand.

Where "putty" or "smooth" finish is specified, material shall be mixed according to directions of the manufacturer.

ROUGH PLASTER SAND FINISH

Rough plaster and cement on all walls and ceilings shall be applied in two coats.

First coat shall be used only to fill our hollows in terra cotta walls and to thickness of ¼" over lath and on plain ceilings.

Second coat shall have a minimum thickness of 5/8" and shall be well pressed on making perfect adhesion with terra cotta and perfect key to all lath.

All plain walls and ceiling plaster shall be run from Plaster of Paris screeds which shall be erected at all corners and angles perfectly plumb and true and in same plane.

After second coat has been applied, screeds shall be entirely removed and space filled with rough plaster.

All rough plaster shall be run back of all trim and wainscot and around all radiators or other recesses and extend down to the cinder fill or rough floor and fill out to all grounds.

This rough plaster shall be applied witn steel trowels and surfaced with floats. All surfaces shall be brought to a true surface with long straight edges.

Before any plaster is applied to terra cotta clocks, they shall be well set.

MIXING & APPLYING SMOOTH FINISH MACOUSTIC

Smooth finish macoustic as delivered in bags is ready for mixing with clear water. Nothing else may be added on the job. A slight excess of water is recommended during a soaking period of one hour. Dry material should then be added to bring the mass to a stiff working consistency. Overnight soaking is not recommended but the mix may be retempered if necessary.

A mechanical plaster mixer if available is recommended.

A brisk hoeing or mixing just before hodding is recommended.

Thickness of smooth finish macoustic - Smooth finish macoustic must be applied a FULL ½" thick - no less, unless otherwise specified.

APPLY SMOOTH FINISH MACOUSTIC OVER ORDINARY GYPSUM OR LIME BROWN MORTAR (BONE-DRY AND WELL SCRATCHED). Apply first a base (scratch) coat of smooth finish Macoustic ¼" thick with a steel trowel. Straighten with a darby and allow to take-up until free water is absorbed from the surface. Then double back and lay on ¼" of the same material with as little trowelling as possible. (Bring up to a true surface with minimum working). ALLOW to take-up again until free water disappears: then DRAG TROWEL OVER THE SURFACE TO ELIMINATE TROWEL MARKS AND TO OPEN UP SURFACE.

SAMPLE PANEL BEFORE STARTING JOB. In order to acquaint your plasterers with the ease and simplicity of Smooth Finish Macoustic application, and the manner in which to secure the desired finish, we recommend that a few shovelfuls of Smooth Finish Macoustic be mixed and applied to some convenient wall space BEFORE STARTING THE JOB. Architect to approve this sample as STANDARD for the job.

JOININGS: Joinings should be avoided wherever possible by running panels and sections in one operation.

DRYING: Smooth Finish Macoustic is a slow drying material, requiring at least ten days to thoroughly dry, depending upon temperature and ventilating conditions. Smooth finish Macoustic becomes progressively harder and stronger for a period of months after application.

DECORATING: The surface of Smooth Finish Macoustic must not be decorated or otherwise treated except in manner approved by manufacturer.

WORKMANSHIP

All walls and ceilings shall be finished perfectly plane and true.

All walls so specified shall be well trowelled down to smooth hard and polished surface with no trowel, brush or other marks showing. All plain walls and ceilings shall be applied in one operation, with no laps.

All moulding shall be run from zinc template cut to accurately fit full size details, which shall be furnished by the Architect.

All walls and ceiling throughout unless otherwise specified are to have a rough plaster finish.

Where offsets or panels occur in walls or ceilings in connection with flat cornices, band courses or other decorative features the plasterer must build out with rough plater, as required by the drawings and where the ribs are deep enough to require it, proper furring with metal lath is to be furnished.

Where an enrichment is shown in any portion of the building the same is to be duplicated on all corresponding parts of the building.

All moulded bands, ribs, cornices, courses, etc. shall be run straight and true with all mitres perfectly formed. All ribs and curved mouldings shall conform to drawings and details.

All corresponding members are to be of uniform depth and width.

All constructional beams which in their dimensions are not as wide or as deep as required in the finished size, must be furred out to the required dimensions with metal straps of approved sizes and metal lath of specified gauge.

LANDINGS & SOFFITS OF STAIRS

Landings and soffits of all stairs are to be included in plaster except where marked unfinished soffit.

MODELS

This Contractor shall include all necessary models, by an artist approved by the Architect, who shall be considered a sub-contractor of this plastering contractor. All models shall be approved by the Architects before casting is done.

Parducci Studios, have extimated this work as directed by Architect. Will furnish quotations.

Models shall be made of all requiring same, both right and left, and this contractor shall make casts for same. Casts must be made fully as sharp as model and if otherwise in Architect's opinion, shall not be used.

All dimensions are for models shall be given by this contractor.

Apply all moulded and enriched members, indicated, caps and ornament of every description, whether specifically mentioned or not.

BASE COAT

The Base and Brown coats for imitation stone shall consist of one part Keene's cement to three parts sand (two parts sand only on metal lath) and shall be applied as before specified for rough plaster.

As soon as brown coat is thoroughly dry paint with one good covering coat of R.I.W.

FINISH COAT

The finish coat of all imitation stone work shall be 3/8" thick. The finish coat shall be made and colored so as to represent as nearly as possible the color and texture of the Natural Stone Wainscot but all stones must vary slightly in color so as to give "Texture" to wall and samples shall be prepared and submitted to the Architects for their approval before any material is shipped to the job.

Great care shall be observed in mixing and applying the material to prevent any foreign matter, which may affect the tone of color from being introduced.

Mortar shall be mixed with clean water according to the directions of the manufacturers, shall be applied by mechanics and thoroughly compressed. The finish shall be floated off to a smooth surface, and when set, but still wet shall be dressed off with a hack saw scraper to remove float marks. Joints up to level of column caps shall be cut out to imitate stone jointed as shown on drawings and shall afterwards be filled in with Keene's Cement. Above the level of column caps joints will be painted on by the contractor for painting. After the whole surface is dry, sandpaper as directed by the Architect. The variation of color shall be obtained by the manipulation of the material.

Run all mouldings as indicated on drawings.

WORKMANSHIP

Contractor for this work shall have an established reputation for this particular class of work and shall demonstrate to the Architect his ability to produce a strictly high-class job by reference to similar work previously done by him and erected not less than three years prior to this date.

All mechanics employed in connection with this work shall be men particularly skilled in the handling and finishing of material in question.

Ordinary plasterers shall not be considered as qualified under the above requirements
and all shall be employed subject to the approval of the architect.

PROTECTION
This contractor shall erect board protection, and keep same in good
order, to all corners and other work, as may be liable to injury, or as directed
by the Architect.

PATCHING
The Contractor shall repair all damaged plastering at such times as the
Architect may direct, but shall be paid for this by the General Contractor
responsible for damage done, as an addition to this contract. Repairs to
damaged initation stone work shall not be done until all other work has been
completed and any damaged stones shall be cut out completely from joint
to joint and entirely replaced.

SCAGLIOLA WORK
All work marked on drawings "Scagliola" including main columns shall
be faced with scagliola with highly polished surface and matching different
veined marbles as directed by the Architect.

All scagliola shall be executed in the best manner by competent workmen
approved by the Architect. The Contractor for this work must be able to refer
to work of similar nature in service sufficient to justify his employment on
this work. High grade of craftsmenship will be demanded.

METAL STRIPS
Strips of metal lath at least 4" wide on each wing and machine broken
in angles, are to be installed at all junctions of tile or gypsite or metal
lath walls with brick walls.

LATHING ADDENDA

METAL CORNER BEADS
All extruding angles shall have heavy 24 Gauge G.I. corner beads from
base to ceiling to be Milcor or Bostwick type.

<u>CARPENTRY WORK</u>

<u>GENERAL CONDITION AND GENERAL CONTRACTOR'S SPECIFICATION
IN THE FRONT OF THESE SPECIFICATION TOGETHER WITH THE FOLLOWING
TO GOVERN THIS WORK.</u>

<u>MEASUREMENTS</u>
All work included in this contract shall be prepared for actual measure-
ments taken at the building by this Contractor.
He shall call the attention of the Architect to any discrepancies between
work as built and as shown on drawings and shall adjust the work to fit the
conditions as the Architect may direct without extra charge.

<u>STORAGE</u>
All rough work shall be stored in a dry shed and all finished work within
the building, properly protected and covered. No finished work shall be brought
into the building until the plaster is thoroughly dry and the written permission
of the Architect has been obtained.

<u>TEMPORARY RUNWAYS & LADDERS</u>
Provide and maintain runways and ladders from lowest level building to
roof, with separate ladders for ascent and descent, for the use of all workmen
on the job, until stairs and permanent ladders are erected.

<u>CENTERING</u>
Provide and set all necessary centering for Mason and Plasterer all strongly
made and braced to sustain their loads, fitting accurately to all parts and
left in place until removal is ordered by the Architects. Also provide all
necessary templates of arches, bays, etc. as required by Mason, stonecutter
or mill to ensure the accurate fitting together of all frames and woodwork
with the Masonry.

<u>ENCLOSING BUILDING</u>
When directed this contractor shall close all exterior door openings of
basement and first floor with temporary doors furnished with strap hinges
padlocks and three keys for each padlock one of which is to be handed to
the Architect's Superintendent.

<u>CUTTING & FITTING</u>
DO all necessary and customary cutting and fitting for the other tradesmen
on the building, cutting away and rebuilding, fitting to other work, cutting
for ducts, registers, pipes etc.

<u>DEFECTS</u>
This contractor shall be responsible for and shall make good all defects
appearing in his work, adjusting of doors, windows etc., at his own expense, for
a period of one year after the last payment is made.

LUMBER IN GENERAL

All lumber shall be sound and as well seasoned as the market affords, and of the kinds and grades as hereafter specified and shall be full and square to the dimensions specified or shown. If commercial sizes be used, the number shall be increased to give a total sectional area equivalent to that shown on plans.

ROUGH LUMBER

All rough lumber for interior work shall be best quality Southern Pine.

JOISTING & RAFTERS

Joisting and rafters shall be of sizes and set at centers as indicated on drawings, cut and fitted to the construction as detailed and where built into wall shall be out with bevelled ends and shall be furnished with strap iron anchors supplied and nailed on by this contractor.

Provide all string pieces and blocking to be bolted to steel where shown or required for carrying joisting or other material as required by detailed drawings.

PLATFORMS

Build platform in basement as indicated with 2" x 6" joist wedged up from concrete slab.

ROOFS

Build main roofs as indicated on drawings, planking of sizes and set as indicated, notched on to oak string pieces and securely spiked. Wall plates shall be as shown on details not less than 2" thick bolted to walls every 30" by means of 5/8" anchor bolts 20" long supplied by this contractor to mason to be built into wall. Oak string pieces shall be bolted to channel purlins and all other steel members carrying joists or rafters by this contractor, the steel contractor shall punch steel for $\frac{1}{2}$" bolts 30" o.c.. All other roofs shall be built as shown, rafters bridged as before specified. All roof surfaces except where planking is used to be covered with No. 1 Common Southern Pine shiplap triple nailed at every bearing with 8-penny common nails. All spaces marked for metal roofing shall be covered with No. 1 Common Southern Pine flooring breadths not over 6" nailed with 8-penny flooring nails, joints dressed after laying. Those surfaces must be left perfectly smooth for roofer, no loose knots will be permitted and all knot-holes or other irregularities shall be cut out neatly a nd smoothly and patched. Joints of shiplap and flooring shall be broken at each board. Build all saddles, curbs, etc. as required and as shown and provide $1\frac{1}{2}$" tilting fillets at all parapets, valleys and flashings. Supply to roofer to be nailed on by him: $2\frac{1}{2}$ x $2\frac{1}{2}$ bevelled strips for all copper covered roofs.

SLEEPERS

In spaces marked for wood floors, which rest directly on concrete slabs, lay 2" x 3" bevelled sleepers 12" o.c. A sleeper shall be laid close to and parrallel with all walls and partitions and all sleeper ends shall be fitted and butted to this, securely nailed. After sleepers are laid they shall be wedged up from the concrete to a true horizontal plane and this contractor shall be responsible for the correct level of finished floor, shall make good at his own expense any defects in sleepers before finished floor is laid.

GROUNDS

Grounds shall be 3/4" x 2" for all stud partitions and wherever metal lath and plaster occur 5/8" x 2" on all tile walls, but shall be increased in size as necessary to carry trim or panelling and where so shown on details.

They shall be nailed to wood stud partitions, secured to tile or brick walls by means of "Ankyra" wall bolts, and wired through gypsite or metal stud partitions. Double grounds shall be run for all wood bases. All grounds shall be put up straight and true and shall be thoroughly secured and rigid before plaster is applied.

FURRING

All furring of exterior walls, pipe chases, etc. will be done by plasterer, but this contractor shall build framing to carry wire lath where necessary and shall provide all blocking pieces, brackets, etc. required for ceilings of aisles, Narthex, etc. and wherever shown on drawings and details.

EXTERIOR FINISH

All wood exposed to weather, all lookouts built into wall to support exterior work shall be Cypress, White or Sugar Pine.

All window frame moldings shall be clear white or Sugar Pine.

EXTERIOR DOOR FRAMES

All door frames will have a wood molding outside and be secured to metal frame as detailed.

ROOF CONSTRUCTION OVER SACRISTIES

Where indicated on plans and sections construct roof framing to conform to the drawings with material of dimensions and size as indicated. Cover with sound No. Common Shiplap roofing.

FLOOR INSULATION

Between all double floor lay a heavy covering of Asbestor paper, completing covering all under floors before finishing floor is laid.

PLATFORMS

Construct frame work for platforms in basement with steps as indicated. This construction to be of 2 x 4 with 2 x 6 joist for floors, properly built to secure sound construction.

RUNWAYS & WALKS

The above work will be a single floor No. 1 Common Shiplap laid over the joist frame work which is to be built as indicated on plans and of dimensioned material as marked on plans.

CAULKING

Before the staff molds are put up and before painting is done, this contractor shall caulk all joints between frame and brickwork with picked oakum, well driven home afterwards replacing the staff moulding. Frames of windows not having staff mouldings shall be covered on backs with pad of oakum $\frac{1}{2}$" thick secured to frames.

MAIN ENTRANCE & VESTIBULE DOORS

Main entrance doors shall be 2-3/4" thick built up of three thicknesses of clear White Oak, put together grain reversed with 3/4" solid panels and raised mouldings, with turned bosses in center of each panel.

Doors shall be put together with while lead and and oil and heavy counter-sunk scres, heads of screws concealed by plugs.

Doors shall have 3/4" wood studs on both sides as shown.

Vestibule doors shall be similar but $2\frac{1}{4}$" thick of two thicknesses of $1\frac{1}{4}$" oak.

Frames are of steel by the Steel Contractor, but Carpenter shall apply hardware and fit and hang doors.

INTERIOR FINISH

All interior finish unless otherwise specified shall be clear red oak thoroughly dried.

INTERIOR DOOR FRAMES

Interior door frames in heavy walls shall be 1-3/4" thick rebated for doors securely anchored to walls in which they occur, in wood or gypsite partitions, they shall be 1-3/8" thick well blocked out from bucks or studs.

TRIM

All mouldings shall be run true straight, in strict accordance with drawings and details, all internal angles coped, external angles mitred. All casings shall rest on bevelled plinth blocks, and shall have joints coped, with mitres on moulding at inner edge and on backband, or backband moulding, where such members occur.

All joints in circular work and in hand rails shall be reinforces and bolted using double and screw bolts for stair rails.

All finish of every kind shall be thoroughly sandpapered and left perfectly smooth, clean and ready for painter.

Trim of Church and Chapel Doors and windows as detailed.

PANELLING

Stiles and rails not otherwise specified or shown shall not be less than 1-1/8" thick with face veneer at least $\frac{1}{4}$" thick unless otherwise specified. Panels shall be 5-ply cross-veneered on pine core or of solid V Jointed tongued and grooved pieces where so indicated. Face veneers shall be of equal thickness on both sides. Panelling shall be delivered to job, assembled in lengths as far as possible. Panelling shall be set up straight and true and secured to grounds so as to hold material securely in place. All panelling shall be filled and shellaced by painter before being assembled.

BACKPAINTING

All trim and panelling shall receive one good coat of linseed oil on back of all finished woodwork of every kind shall be filled stained or pimed by the painter, before it is put together, and this contractor shall notify painter when trim is ready and shall afford all facilities to painter for the performance of his work.

INTERIOR DOORS

All interior doors unless otherwise specified shall be double faced of the best kiln dried material, stiles and rails veneered in clear red oak on staved up pine core. Veneers shall be specially selected for grain and color. Basement door panels shall be $\frac{1}{2}$" thick of solid V jointed pieces in narrow breadths as indicated on design and detail, all breadths equal in say one door. All other panels shall be of ply veneer. All doors shall be guaranteed against warping, shrinking or other bad workmanship. They shall be equipped with hardware as hereafter specified and shall be properly balanced and hung, swinging with uniformly fitting joint around frame making opening end tight as near as possible, without binding. They shall be of dimensions and designs as indicated on drawings, not less than 1-3/4" thick unless otherwise specified, and where so marked shall be divided with muntins and provided with glass stops and loose moulding.

TOILER ROOM SCREEN

Toiler room screens and partitions shall be 13/16" thick oak ceiling breadths not over 4" with V joints with stiles and rails $2\frac{1}{2}$" x 3" grooved for reception of ceiling boards and supported on 1" x 12" pipe standards with $2\frac{1}{2}$" flanges bolted to floor and secured to partitions with long wood screws. This Contractor shall furnish and erect 1" steel pipe head rail passing through head of posts. Heads of posts shall be shaped as detailed.

TOILET STALL DOORS

Toilet Stall doors shall be 1-1/8" thick with plain panels all as shown and detailed, hung on Carpenter's patent gravity hinges and furnished with latches and bumpers.

BALCONY

Panelling of balcony front and soffit also brackets shall be built upon backing of 2" x 4" studs set 16" o.c.. Securely nailed and braced to the wood joisting floor.

Panel stiles and rails shall be 1-1/8" thick, panels of 5-ply veneer, mouldings and cap built as detailed, back of $\frac{1}{2}$" V jointed oak ceiling.

CONFESSIONALS

Build the confessionals as indicated on drawings and as detailed. Fronts and doors shall be 1-3/4" thick built as specified previously for rails. Provide 1-3/8" moulded edged benches supported on stout brackets. Ceiling shall be built and panelled as indicated, this contractor shall set the metal grilles in doors, ceilings, etc. provided by contractor for miscellaneous iron.

All openings and pierced work of doors and front shall be provided with screens of fine mesh bronze wire stretched tightly secured with mouldings. Provide sliding latticed panels on each side of central compartment on the inside of lattice, all as shown on details.

SHRINES

At each end of transepts build shrines and radiator fronts as indicated on drawings with plasters, cornice and composition ornament where shown. Grilles on radiator recesses are of iron by contractor for Miscellaneous Iron.

COMPOSITION ORNAMENT

Supply and install all composition ornament shown on drawings, including all enriched mouldings, twisted columns, caps and grilles so marked. Models of all ornament shall be made and approved by the Architect before any work is done. A composition work shall be of first rate material and workmanship grained to imitate oak.

MUSIC CABINET

Build music cabinet shelves as indicated in recesses and detailed with curtain pole at top for curtain which will be furnished by others.

CASINGS

All doors in partitions, all windows with inside casings that are in line with inner side of wall in which they occur, and all openings so indicated on drawings shall have 3½" casing, with 1-1/8" x 7/8" backband, all casings shall have coped and mitred joints, shall have heads shaped carefully to detail and shall be supported on bevelled plinth blocks. Door frames in walls over 6" thick shall have staff mouldings only.

WOOD BASE

Cement floors shall have cement bases. All wood floors shall have 3/4" x 8" moulded bases coped at angles, and finished with floor shoe all as detailed. Double grounds shall be run for all bases. This does not apply to large room of basement which whill have 8" wood base.

CAP MOULDINGS

Run wood cap mouldings 3/4" x 3" at wainscot in toilets and wherever shown on drawings, and run 7/8" x 2" picture moulding in Sacristies and passage.

WARDROBES & VESTMENT CABINETS

Build these cabinets as shown and detailed with 1-3/8" ends, tops and fronts, rabbitted for doors, 7/8" panelled doors and ½" V jointed ceiling.

Drawers shall have 3/4" backs, ½" sides and 3-ply veneered bottoms.

HANDRAIL

Provide moulded oak handrail for iron stairs also pound rail at walls on all sides of stairs. All joints shall be reinforced with double and counter sunk screw bolts and wood shall be secured to iron with long wood screws, counter sunk on under side of iron.

Provide wall round rails to all stairs carried on cast iron handrail brackets securely anchor bolted through construction. Expansion bolts wood screws or plugs will not be permitted except in old work now standing.

ROUGH FLOORS

Overlay all joist for wood flooring with No. 1 Common S. Pine Shiplap, triple nailed at each bearing.

FINISHED FLOORS OF GALLERY

Floors of Choir Gallery shall have finished floors of 13/16 x 2" clear oak flooring thoroughly kiln dried, blind nailed and not over 12" o.c. with 8-penny floor nails, dressed, scraped and sanded and left ready for painter, free from all defects, too or sander marks.

All finished wood floors shall be laid on one thickness heavy asbestos paper lapping joints at least 3".

HATCHES
Provide wood hatches for access to tower floors and all otherwise inaccessible ceiling spaces where indicated.

<u>HARDWARE SPECIFICATION</u>

The Contractor shall furnish and apply all hardware required to make a complete and finished job including rough and finished hardware. The numbers referred to in the following specification are taken from the catalogue of Yale & Towne Mfg. Co. unless otherwise specified, except the butts which shall be of Stanley make.

Hardware of similar design and quality but of other manufacture may be substituted subject to the approval of the architect. All hardware shall be delivered to the building with each piece or group properly wrapped and marked for the openings on which it is to be used.

The following specification is intended to cover the type of hardware to be used but any hardware not specifically mentioned therein yet necessary to complete the work shall be furnished by the contractor.

FINISH FOR THE SERVICE PORTION to be genuine bower barff.

TOILETS to be polished nickel plated on solid brass.

BALANCE OF HARDWARE IN THE BASEMENT to be as Yale's BY23.

BALANCE OF DOORS IN THE MAIN PORTION to be BY23.

MAIN ENTRANCE DOORS to have the following: BUTTS BB 181 6 x 6 Four to & leaf. MORTISE FLUSH BOLTS #63-12" and 18". DOOR HOLDER 831½ Yale Closers #76 with corner bracket for each leaf. Monarch exit devices, 1000P x 1001 kick plates.

VESTIBULE DOORS to have butts BB-241, 6 x 6 four to a leaf. Yale closers 175 one to each leaf. Pulls 727. Monarch, Push Plates GS 1730 - 3½ x 16 and kick plates.

SINGLE EXIT DOORS to be furnished with Monarch's exit devices 1000 and pairs of exit doors with 1000P x 1001.

DOUBLE ACTING DOOR IN BASEMENT with Bommer 7-inch D.A. jamb hinges, Push Plate GS 1730-3½ x 16. Door Holder. Deadlock 324¼.

TOILET ROOM DOORS Lockset same as other interior doors but with close #73.

TOILET STALL DOORS Rommer S.A. Hingers 2108. Bolts 5010. Strikes 10" Hooks 5034. Pulls 2742 Ives.

BALANCE OF INTERIOR DOORS to have 3 butts 241½ - 4½ x 4½, each leaf. Lockset DY 8205 x BY23/

DOORS LEADING FROM STAIR HALL to have 3 butts 241½ - 4½ x 4½ for each leaf. Push & Pull plates and closers.

CABINETS IN SACRISTIES AND BAPTISTRY to be provided with butts of size as required by details. All door 1-1/8" or less to not over 1-3/8" to have butts 3 x 3. All doors 4 ft. high and over to have 3 butts each. Each door and drawer to be provided with pin tumbler cylinder locks to suit thickness of wood as Yale's # 561; all to be master-keyed as directed. Each door in addition to have knob as Yale's and each drawer to have 2 pulls as Yale's G-1074. FURNISH 3 Master Bitt keys and 3 Master Cylinder Keys.

PAINTING

THE GENERAL CONDITIONS AND GENERAL CONTRACTOR'S SPECIFICA-
TIONS IN THE FRONT OF THESE SPECIFICATIONS TOGETHER WITH THE
FOLLOWING TO GOVERN THIS WORK.

GENERAL

The work under this contract includes the painting and finishing of all
wood and metal work, of every kind exterior and interior, whether mentioned
specifically hereinafter or not.

MATERIALS

Paints shall be Truscon, Sherwin and Williams or Dibble.
Varnishes: Berry Bros. Murphy or Standard.
Enamels: Archemik, Sherwin & Williams or equal.

DELIVERY OF MATERIAL

All materials shall be delivered well in advance of the date at which
they are required for use, and in quantities sufficient to permit of the rapid
execution of the work.

When so required, the contractor shall submit bills of material as may
be necessary to enable the Architect to definitely determine the brand and
quality of material used.

All materials shall be delivered to the building in unbroken sealed cans
or packages and shall be opened in the presence of the Architect or his
representative and no adulteration shall be permitted, material being used as
taken from can or package without any addition whatsoever.

All materials shall be subject to the approval of the Architects and the
contractor shall submit for their approval the name of the namufacturer and
the brand and quality of the materials he proposes to use, before ordering any.

No material other than that approved shall be delivered to the building.

OIL

All oil shall be pure linseed thoroughly aged and settled. Raw oil shall
contain no additions of any kind. Boiled oil shall contain only such additions
of lead and manganese driers as may be absorbed by the oil in heating.

LEAD

All white lead shall be pure "Dutch Process" carbonate of lead, free
from acid and subject to approval as to color and manufacture.

COLORS

All colors shall be pure pigments of the best quality and Standard Brands
ground in pure linseed oil.

FILLERS

All fillers for open grain surfaces, unless otherwise specified, shall be
composed of finely ground silica, pure linseed oil and a good quality of Japan
drier, and unless otherwise specified shall be mixed to the consistency of paste.

SHELLAC

Shellac shall be pure white gum cut in alcohol.

TURPENTINE

Turpentine shall be absolutely pure without the addition of any sharp cutting medium. No substitute shall be used.

VARNISH

All varnish shall be of the best quality and manufacture offered by the maker for the class of work for which it is to be used.

Varnish shall be made exclusively from the best quality of hard varnish gum, pure linseed oil, pure turpentine, and the necessary lead and manganese driers, and shall be free from naptha, rosin, or any other adulterant or foreign matter.

The varnish shall not flash in a temperature below 10% degrees Fahr. open tester, shall set to touch in from 6 to 8 hours and dry hard to recoat in 50 hours, all counted from time of completion in a temperature of 70° F.

PAINT

All paint shall be thoroughly mixed in proportions as will best suit the work for which it is required, shall be thoroughly strained, with all color completely and evenly incorporated giving uniform tint and shade.

SAMPLES

The painter shall prepare samples showing color and finish for all portions of the work as directed by the Architect. Completed work shall conform in all respects to samples.

WORKMANSHIP

All materials shall be applied by skilled mechanics in the best fashion. All paint shall be evenly spread, and well brushed out; varnish shall be smoothly and evenly flowed on, without excess of liquid, and all completed surfaces shall show a uniform even face free from all drops, saggs of material and runs or brush marks. No cost of paint, varnish or wax shall be applied until previous coat is thoroughly dry.

CLEANING

Before material is applied to any work, the entire surface shall be cleaned and properly sanded smooth. This process shall be repeated before the application of every additional coat and the completed work shall be left clean and free from dirt, finger marks, rough spots or other defects.

BACKPAINTING & PRIMING

All finished woodwork exterior or interior shall receive one heavy coat of linseed oil on all concealed surfaces.

All woodwork specified for paint shall receive a priming coat of lead and oil sufficiently thin to permit of free absorption. Special care shall be taken to paint the ravvits of all sash before any glazing is done.

All hardwood finish shall be filled or stained and shellaced, before being shipped, and panelling shall be filled, stained or painted before being assembled.

Backpainting, priming and filling shall be done at the mill before material is shipped, and the carpenter shall afford all facilities to painter for the proper execution of his work and shall notify him when material is ready.

EXTERIOR WORK

All exterior work and iron work of every kind, except oak doors and copper work shall receive three coats oil paint including the priming coat.

Clean, touch up and recoat all existing work of basement and boiler house to match the new work.

INTERIOR WORK

Interior woodwork in General is of Oak, except window frames and sash which are of Pine.

All interior pine finish shall receive 3 coats oil paint including priming coat.

All interior oak finish, and including the exterior doors shall receive one coat paste filler colored as directed, wiped off across the grain, and three coats Berry Bros. Liquid Granite.

WOOD FLOORS

All oak floors shall be treated as above specified for oak woodwork.

PROTECTION OF FLOORS

This contractor shall protect all finished floors by means of paper and boarding and on completion shall turn same over to owners in perfect condition.

INTERIOR IRON WORK

All interior iron work, stiars, ladders, grilles, gates, etc. and including tinelad doors shall receive two coats oil paint.

EXTERIOR METAL PAINT

All exterior metal shall be painted one coat of genuine aluminum paint over the metal paint previously applied by other Contractor and finished with two coats of paint. Colors as directed. This includes metal of all windows on building.

GILDING

The entire surfaces of the upper small domes of towers of church and the cross finial of Chapel are to be gilded with genuine Gold Leaf 23 Carat over copper. The specification of manufacturer to be followed for its application. No Dutch metal will be permitted.

<u>GLASS & GLAZING</u>

<u>THE GENERAL CONDITIONS AND GENERAL CONTRACTOR'S SPECIFICA-
TIONS IN THE FRONT OF THESE SPECIFICATIONS TOGETHER WITH THE
FOLLOWING TO GOVERN THIS WORK.</u>

SCOPE OF WORK
       The work covered by this contract comprises the furnishing and setting
of all glass throughout the building, except the inner decorative glass in church
windows.

SAMPLES
       Samples 2' x 2' of all glass to be used shall be submitted to the Architect
for approval and all glass shall conform in every way to the approved samples.

CLEANING
       After all other work is completed, or when directed by the Architects,
the Contractor shall thoroughly clean all glass furnished and set under this
contract.

BROKEN GLASS
       Repairing of damage to glass from any cause shall be done by this
contractor immediately upon notification of the Architect. The cost of this
shall be paid for by the General Contractor, or the contractor responsible
for any dame done, as an addition to this contract.

PUTTYING
       All glass exposed to weather is to be thoroughly back puttied, bradded,
bedded and puttied, and glazing chips shall be used for holding the storm
glass of church windows.

DESCRIPTION OF GLASS
       All glass in the buildings shall be White Cathedral, leaded in panes as
indicated on drawings.
       Leads shall be reinforced with hard brass cores and in large windows shall
not be less than 5/8" wide and shall be reinforced with heavy metal T bars
as indicated.
       All windows with leaded glass shall show a margin of metal beyond the
stop or the putty line equal in breadth to the muntin bars.
       All glass shall be set in the leads with an approved brand of glazing cement.

VENTILATORS
       The ventilating section at bottom of all windows shall be so arranged
and constructed as to operate properly and conveniently with the inside Art
Glass section of ventilator, when the leaded glass windows are installed.

MISCELLANEOUS GLASS
       Three windows of tower 1st floor to be of leaded glass to cost $6.00
per foot. Designs as approved by the Architect. Glass of 4 windows in second
floor towers to remain or to be replaced in new frames if such are required.

Glass in these windows must be repaired or replaced as necessary to match that now in the windows.

Eight small slit windows upper tower to remian if undamaged. Where damaged or broken replace with double rolled Cathedral tinted glass which in all eight windows is to be of uniform type.

All glass in basement to be cathedral double rolled Ambor Glass to match samples approved by Architect or Pastor.

<u>MARBLE TILE & TERRAZZO WORK</u>

<u>THE GENERAL CONDITIONS AND GENERAL CONTRACTOR'S SPECIFICA-
TION IN THE FRONT OF THESE SPECIFICATIONS TOGETHER WITH THE
FOLLOWING TO GOVERN THIS WORK.</u>

GENERAL
Omitted from figure: Steps to altar, marble in Sanctuary, Altar Railing or STatues are not included under this contact.

The supply of all other marble stone and tile and terrazzo work shown on the srawings is to be included and the settings of same as hereunder specified.

TILE WORK
NARTHEX: Tile floor 70¢ per square foot installed. Floor to be a Romany quarry tile or equal with border and body in selected colors and sizes forming Romanesque pattern as determined.

BAPTISTRY: 1 tile floor estimated at $1.15 per square foot. This tile floor to be of Polychrome Flints as manufactured by the Franklin Tile Co. or equal in accordance with selection in selected pattern and color using ecclestical glazed inserts as selected.

AISLES OF NAVE: Tile floor to be estimated 75¢ per square foot. This includes Textone mosaic of border and body in design and color as selected, making sufficient allowance for inserts and border in accordance with design.

CHAPEL: Tile floor and steps to be estimated at !.20 per square foot. This includes tile floor and aisles of Polychrome Flints or equal in border and body design as selected together with ecclestical glazed inserts to form pattern; also, includes tiles for 3 risers of steps leading form Church into Chapel.

All these tiles to be of select quality and to be carried through archways and into door entrances to meet adjoining floors; to be installed in the best workmanlike manner and left clean when finished.

The prices quoted herein are to be used as an outside price for purpose of estimate. The figures as submitted must be in a lump sum amount. Tile other than that specified will be considered but must be of equal quality to that specified.

MARBLE OF CRYPT
The facing of stiles and rails of crypt is to be on $1\frac{1}{4}$" Vermont Green Veined Marble. Sample to be furnished and approved before material is shipped. The face slabs of all crypts are to be 2" thick.

The slab faces of the Crypts which are to be permanently closed will be sealed in with cement over the concrete slab facing, balance set in without sealing up. Each of three crypts is to have incised lettering cut into face of slab corresponding with that in present slabs of old vault which will be discarded. Each inscription comprises about 50 words. Letters $1\frac{1}{4}$" in height and each finished in Dutch Metal Gold Leaf. After carving is done the Pastor is to approve lettering before work is commenced. This contractor to include gilding of letters in his contract.

<u>LINOLEUM FLOORS</u>

<u>THE GENERAL CONDITIONS AND GENERAL CONTRACTOR'S SPECIFICA-
TION IN THE FRONT OF THESE SPECIFICATIONS TOGETHER WITH THE
FOLLOWING TO GOVERN THIS WORK.</u>

<u>GENERAL</u>
This contract includes the laying and waxing of linoleum floors on surface
of all spaces under pews in Church and Chapel.

<u>MATERIAL</u>
Linoleum shall be ARMSTRONG U.S. NAVY STANDARD WALTON Process
Brown or Grey battleship 3/16" thick.

<u>SAMPLES</u>
Two samples of the linoleum on which the bid is based shall be submitted
for the approval of the Architect, and all linoleum furnished must be equal to
the approved samples one of which will be retained by the Architect.

<u>CEMENT</u>
The cement used in securing the Linoleum to the floor shall be one of the
following brands:
    For cementing body of the Linoleum (Non-waterproof)
    Armstrong's Linoleum Paste
    Sisks Lino-Teck
    Gold SEal Linoleum Paste
    Keystone Linoleum Cement
    Glu-tite Linoleum Paste
    Manayunk Stickum
    For cementing seams and edges (Waterproof)
    Armstrong's Waterproof Linoleum Cement
    Gold Seal Waterproof Linoleum Cement
    20th Century Linoleum Glue Cement
    Atlas Super Cement
    The cement must be shipped to the job in the manufacturer's original
package.

<u>WORKMANSHIP</u>
Before commencing work the Contractos shall inspect the under floors
and satisfy himself as to their condition and in the event of finding any defects
shall report same to the General Contractor and the Architect, and shall see
that all are made good before starting his work.

<u>GUARANTEE</u>
The Linoleum Contractor shall guarantee his work to the Owner or the
General Contracotr, as directed by the Architects against defects of material or
workmanship for a period of 5 years from date of acceptance by the Architect,
and shall on reccipt of written notice from the Owner, make at his own expense,
any repairs that may be necessary, except repairs of injury from any cause other
than ordinary wear and tear, and shall furnish a surety bond in the full amount
of the contract covering the performance of this guarantee.

<u>MISCELLANEOUS ADDENDA</u>

CROSSES
　　　　G-Iron - The crosses on main front gable and dome of Chapel are to be
of 16 oz. copper carried out in accordance with the details.

KALAMINE DOOR
　　　　Between Boiler Room and School, provide a 1-3/4" Kalamine Door, conforming
to Fire Underwriters Requirements.
　　　　Channel frame to be provided by Iron Contractor.

CROSS SUPPORTS
　　　　Erect and properly anchor in Masonry on base structure, galvanized steel
channels in size as approved by Superintendent for proper support of copper
crosses.

STEEL DOORS
　　　　Provide Sacristy Vault with Steel Vault Door of 3/8" metal on $2\frac{1}{2}$" base.
Door to be provided with Diebolt or equal combustion lock. The steel frame
to be of angle iron and plate.

IRON GATES & ORNAMENTAL IRON RAILING
　　　　Crypt to vestibule (Double gates)
　　　　Vestibule to basement stair #2, single gate.
　　　　Baptistry, single gate
　　　　Two stationary W.I. Grilles from Sanctuary to Ambulatory
　　　　Double gates from Chapel to Vestibule
　　　　W.I. Ornamental railing at Chap Sanctuary
　　　　W.I. Ornamental railing at Chapel Organ Loft
　　　　All swinging gates to be provided with locks and according to details
as shown and approved shop drawings.

PULPIT
　　　　Not included under main contract but anchorage to column must be
provided for same as hereafter detailed.
　　　　Structural Steel Contractor to provide this under his contract.
　　　　Provide and install channel iron frame for Kalamine Door between Boiler
Room and School.

HARDWARE
　　　　The General Contractor shall allow $1,000.00 in bid to cover all finishing
hardware. All building and construction hardware is to be included in main bid.

GENERAL CELOTEX
　　　　This Contractor is to provide 1" x 2" wood cross furring for 1" Perforated
Celotex tile where joist construction occurs on ceiling of Community Room in
Basement. Plaster on concrete slabs and concrete beams by Plastering Contractor.

METAL LATHING
　　　　Including door and window jambs. Suspended Plaster ceiling in toilets on
basement floor. Suspended Plaster ceiling in recesses in Community Room.

CARPENTRY
    Also include Boys Sacristy, Club Room and Ambulatory.

MASONRY
    On all exterior exposed, work, mastic cement should be applied with
pressure gun with approval of Architect.

STONE
    All sandstone as specified or shown together with the sandstone trimmings
of present church, is to be given a rust colored stain at completion of the work
and after this stone is pointed. This stone shall be stained with a Stone Stain,
formula as hereafter approved.

STEEL WINDOW FRAMES
    Provide and install all metal window frames for all circular head windows
in Church and Chapel excepting the windows of towers which will be wood frames.

CARPENTRY
    All window frames of the two towers of Main Church will be of wood.
Majority of these windows 16 in all are in good condition. Any repairs or
replacements must be made as required by Superintendent. This may apply
to 6 of 8 frames. See elevations.

TABLE III

CAR #CDW 43162 INVOICE

FROM

THE HUTTER CONSTRUCTION COMPANY

THE HUTTER CONSTRUCTION CO.
BUILDERS
136 WESTERN AVENUE
PHONE 712
FOND DU LAC, WISCONSIN

DATE Aug. 18, 1836

TERMS Net

CONST. NO 3625

LD TO   St. Peter's Cathedral

Marquette, Michigan

INVOICE NO. 1131

CAR NO. CGW 43162

RETAIN THIS BILL AS IT IS THE ONLY ITEMIZED BILL YOU WILL RECEIVE. IF NOT CORRECT PLEASE NOTIFY US AT ONCE **Page 1.**

REG. NO.	DAY	ITEMS		CHARGES		CREDITS	BALANCE
		2 – Straight Edges	@ $ .75	$ 1	50		
		150 ft. Air Hose	@ .22	33	00		
		300 ft. 1/2" Cable	@ .112	33	60		
		400 ft. 1/2" Cable	@ .112	44	80		
		500 ft. No. 14 Wire		5	00		
		500 ft. No. 8 Wire		13	00		
		500 ft. No. 6 Wire		23	50		
		200 ft. Rubber Covered Wire	@ .25	50	00		
		6 Wood Rollers	@ 1.00	6	00		
		6 Pipe Rollers	@ .25	1	50		
		14 pcs. 2x10-16 – 373 ft.	@ 20.00	7	46		
		2 – 2 wheel trucks	@ 7.50	15	00		
		7 pcs. 4x4-9)					
		7 " 4x4-8) 159 ft.	@ 20.00	3	18		
		4 Bottle Jacks	@ 5.00	20	00		
		3 Axe Handles	@ .50	1	50		
		6 Sledge Hammer Handles	@ .60	3	60		
		8 Hammer Handles	@ .35	2	80		
		1500 ft. Guy Line	@ .04	60	00		
		60 – 5/8" Cable Clips	@ .55	33	00		
		60 – 1/2" Cable Clips	@ .48	28	80		
		60 – 3/8" Cable Clips	@ .36	19	60		
		1 – Tarpaulin – 13x14 – 182 sq. ft.					
		1 " 13x16 – 208 "					
		1 " 12x14 – 168 "					
		1 " 11x16 – 176 "					
		1 " 10x14 – 140 "					
		1 " 10x12 – 120 "					
		1 " 14x16 – 224 "					
		1 " 12x17 – 204 "					
		1 " 10x12 – 120 "					
		1 " 8x16 – 128 "					
		1 " 14x16 – 224 "					
		1 " 8x18 – 144 "					
		1 " 14x17 – 238 "					
		1 " 14x16 – 224 "					
		1 " 11x13 – 145 "					
		1 " 14x16 – 224 "					
		1 " 12x14 – 168 "					
		k " 13x16 – 208 "					
		1 " 10x12 – 120 "					
		1 " 10x16 – 160 " 3523 sq. ft.		140	92		

THE HUTTER CONSTRUCTION CO.
BUILDERS
136 WESTERN AVENUE
PHONE 712
FOND DU LAC, WISCONSIN

DATE Aug. 18, 1936

TERMS Net

CONST. NO 3625

_D TO   St. Peter's Cathedral

Marquette, Michigan

INVOICE NO. 1131

CAR NO. G&W 45162

RETAIN THIS BILL AS IT IS THE ONLY ITEMIZED BILL YOU WILL RECEIVE. IF NOT CORRECT PLEASE NOTIFY US AT ONCE

REG. NO.	DAY	ITEMS		CHARGES	CREDITS	BALANCE
		Brought forward:		$ 547 76		
		4 pcs. 6x8-10 Timbers 160 ft.)				
		4 " 8x8-10 " 213 ") 373 ft. @ $25.00	$	9 42		
		1 - Bull Punch		1 00		
		1200 ft. 7/8" Rope	@ .04½	54 00		
		12 - 40 W. Bulbs)				
		12 - 60 W. Bulbs)		3 60		
		50 ft. Light Wire				
		1 - Hack Saw		50		
		1 - 8" Crescent Wrench		85		
		1 - 12" Crescent Wrench		1 25		
		1 - 12" Pipe Wrench		1 50		
		1 - Screw Driver		25		
		1 - Plumb Bob		25		
		2 - Cason Buckets	@ 10.00	20 00		
		1 - First Aid Cot		5 00		
		10 - Water Hose Gaskets		25		
		6 - Hose Clamps	@ .05	30		
		3 pr. Hose Couplings	@ .10	30		
		13 - Turnbuckles - 18"	@ 1.50	19 50		
		16 - Turnbuckles - 36"	@ 2.00	32 00		
		12 - Turnbuckles - 18"	@ 1.50	18 00		
		1 - Roll 5/8" Cable - 350 ft.	@ .14	49 00		
		1 - Roll 1/2" Cable - 500 ft.	@ .112	56 00		
		2 pcs. 3/8" Cable - 600 ft.	@ .09	54 00		
		4 - 2"x2"x8" Carborundum Stones	@ 2.50	10 00		
		3 - 3"x3"x8" " "	@ 3.50	10 50		
		6 - old pieces	@ 1.00	6 00		
		2 - Heavy Warehouse Brooms	@ 1.00	2 00		
		1 - Light Office Broom		75		
		2 - Wire Nippers	@ 1.25	2 50		
		10 - Mortar Wheelbarrows	@ 5.00	50 00		
		10 - Brick Wheelbarrows	@ 5.00	50 00		
		1 - Heavy 4-Wheel Truck		12 00		
		2 - Timber Dollies for steel	@ 6.50	13 00		
		2 - Dollies	@ 5.00	10 00		
		6 pcs. 3/4" or 7/8" Rope - 1200 ft.	@ .04	48 00		
		4 " 150 ft. Rope - 600 ft.	@ .04	24 00		
		10 - No. 2 Concrete Breakdown Shovels	@ 1.25	12 50		
		12 - rd. pt. Long Handle Shovels		16 50		
		5 - Scoops #3	@ 1.35	6 85		
		12 - Picks	@ 1.50	18 00		
		15 - Pick Handles	@ .50	7 50		
		Carried forward:		$1,174 83		

THE HUTTER CONSTRUCTION CO.
BUILDERS
136 WESTERN AVENUE
PHONE 712
FOND DU LAC, WISCONSIN

DATE Aug. 18, 1936

TERMS Net

CONST. NO 3625

SOLD TO   St. Peter's Cathedral

Marquette, Michigan

INVOICE NO 1131

CAR NO. G&W 43162

RETAIN THIS BILL AS IT IS THE ONLY ITEMIZED BILL YOU WILL RECEIVE. IF NOT CORRECT PLEASE NOTIFY US AT ONCE **Page 3.**

REG. NO.	DAY	ITEMS		CHARGES $1,174 83		CREDITS		BALANCE
		6 – Digging Spaces	@ $1.50	$ 9	00			
		2 – Sand Scoops	@ 1.50	3	00			
		3 – Long Handle Sq.Pt. Shovels	@ 1.25	3	75			
		3 – Snatch Blocks	@ 10.00	30	00			
		4 pr. Rubber Boots, size 10	@ 3.50	14	00			
		6 – Rain Coats	@ 1.50	9	00			
		6 – Rain Hats	@ .50	3	00			
		4 pcs. Chain – medium – 50 ft.	@ .20	10	00			
		6 pcs. Chain – heavy – 98 ft.	@ .20	19	80			
		1 Box Assorted Bolts & Washers		5	00			
		3 – Steel Mortar Boxes	@ 10.00	30	00			
		2 – Step Ladders	@ 2.50	5	00			
		2 – Water Tanks	@ 5.00	10	00			
		2 – 1 gal. Oil Cans	@ .60	1	20			
		2 – 5 gal. Oil Cans	@ .90	1	80			
		1 Small Oil Can			25			
		10 Wrecking Bars	@ .85	8	50			
		18 – Hammers	@ .75	13	50			
		6 – Crow Bars – assorted	@ 2.50	15	00			
		3 – Large Mortar Hoes	@ 1.75	5	25			
		3 – Small Mortar Hoes	@ 1.25	3	75			
		4 pr. Brick Tongs	@ 2.00	8	00			
		3 – Sledge Hammers, 8-10 & 12#	@ 3.00	9	00			
		2 – sq.face Busting Hammers for stone	@ 5.00	10	00			
		2 – Roller Sand Screens	@ .50	1	00			
		3 – Bottle Jacks	@ 5.00	15	00			
		1 – Ler Jack		7	50			
		6 – 5 lb. Pails Grease – 30 lbs.	@ .15	4	50			
		2 – Alemite Grease Guns	@ 1.50	3	00			
		1 – 5 gal. Can IsoVis #30	@ .55	3	30			
		1 – 5 gal. Can for air line lubricator		3	30			
		6 – Points	@ 2.25	13	25			
		200 ft. 1" Water Pipe	@ .10	20	00			
		300 ft. Water Hose, Gaskets & Clamps	@ .09	27	00			
		2 gal. Electric Switch Oil	@ 1.00	2	00			
		2 gal. Steam Cylinder Oil	@ 1.00	2	00			
		1 Concrete Spade		1	75			
		2 Short Spades	@ 1.25	2	50			
		1 Rake		1	00			
		6 – Chisels	@ .50	3	00			
		4 – 2# Mash Hammers	@ 1.00	4	00			
		3 – 2½# or 3# Mash Hammers	@ 1.00	3	00			

THE HUTTER CONSTRUCTION CO.
BUILDERS
136 WESTERN AVENUE
PHONE 712
FOND DU LAC, WISCONSIN

DATE Aug. 18, 1936

TERMS Net

CONST. NO 3625

OLD TO St. Peter's Cathedral

Marquette, Michigan

INVOICE NO 1131

RETAIN THIS BILL AS IT IS THE ONLY ITEMIZED BILL YOU WILL RECEIVE. IF NOT CORRECT PLEASE NOTIFY US AT ONCE Page 4

REG. NO.	DAY	ITEMS		CHARGES		CREDITS	BALANCE
		Brought forward:		$1,519	73		
		2 – Hand Axes	@ $1.25	2	50		
		2 – Axes	@ 1.25	2	50		
		1 – Forge – complete		30	00		
		1 – Anvil		12	00		
		1 – Bench Vise		17	50		
		1 – Cross Cut Saw		3	50		
		2 – Hand Saws	@ 1.50	3	00		
		2 – Lewis Pins with chains	@ 1.50	3	00		
		6 – Lewis Pins without chains	@ 1.00	6	00		
		1 – Complete Set and Wrench		2	00		
		2 – Crescent Wrenches	@ 1.25	2	50		
		1 – 24" Pipe Wrench		2	25		
		2 – 18" Pipe Wrenches	@ 1.75	3	50		
		1 – 18" Pipe Wrench		1	75		
		2 – Monkey Wrenches	@ 1.50	3	00		
		1 – No. 2 Cutter for cutting pipe		3	50		
		2 – Hack Saw Frames	@ .50	1	00		
		20 – Balls Mason Twine	@ .20	4	00		
		12 – Balls Blue Chalk			30		
		1 pr. Hinges			10		
		5 – Hasps	@ .15		75		
		1 – Pint Measure			15		
		1 – 1 gal. Measure			40		
		1 – 2 qt. Measure (oil)			75		
		2 doz. New Pails	@ 7.80	15	60		
		1 doz. Old Pails		6	00		
		1 Wheelbarrow Chain		2	50		
		4 – Saw Horses	@ 1.00	4	00		
		3 – Ladders	@ 6.00	18	00		
		2 – Rolls Friction Tape	@ .15		30		
		5 – Hose Clamps	@ .10		50		
		Hose Gaskets			10		
		1 – Nozzle			50		
		6 – 12" Flat Files	@ .10		60		
		6 – 18" Files	@ .15		90		
		3 – Brooms	@ .75	2	25		
		10 – Salamanders	@ 3.00	30	00		
		1 – Water Kettle		10	00		
		10 – Light Sockets	@ .20	2	00		
		2 – Extension Cords – 25' & 50'	@ 1.25 & 2.50	3	75		
		315 ft. Extra Wire No. 14		3	15		
		Carried forward:		$1,725	83		

THE HUTTER CONSTRUCTION CO.
BUILDERS
136 WESTERN AVENUE
PHONE 712
FOND DU LAC, WISCONSIN

DATE Aug. 18, 1936

TERMS Net

CONST. N 5625

SOLD TO St. Peter's Cathedral

Marquette, Michigan

INVOICE NO. 1131

CAR C&G 43162

RETAIN THIS BILL AS IT IS THE ONLY ITEMIZED BILL YOU WILL RECEIVE. IF NOT CORRECT PLEASE NOTIFY US AT ONCE   Page 5

REG. NO.	DAY	ITEMS		CHARGES		CREDITS	BALANCE
		Brought forward:		$1,725	83		
		310 ft. Extra Wire No. 12		$ 3	10		
		50 ft. No. 14 Wire			50		
		3 – Wire Twisters	@ $1.25	3	75		
		2 – Double Sockets			50		
		6 – 30 amp. Fuses	@ .05		30		
		6 – Male & Female Plugs	@ .05		30		
		2 pr. Steel Tongs	@ 10.00	20	00		
		2 pr. Stone Tongs	@ 12.00	24	00		
		1 pc. Rope 3/4", 24'	@ .05	1	20		
		1 pc. Rope & Blocks 1", 175'		15	00		
		1 pc. Rope 1", 50 ft.	@ .05	2	50		
		1 pc. Rope 1", 28 ft.	@ .05	1	40		
		1 pc. Rope 1", 36 ft.	@ .05	1	80		
		1 pc. Rope 3/4", 15 ft.	@ .04	.	60		
		1 pc. Rope 1", 120 ft.	@ .05	6	00		
		1 pc. Rope 1", 95 ft.	@ .05	4	75		
		1 pc. Rope 1", 150 ft.	@	7	50		
		1 pc. Rope 1", 210 ft.		10	50		
		1 pc. Rope 1", 220 ft.		11	00		
		1 pc. Rope 1", 110 ft.		5	50		
		1 pc. Rope 1", 85 ft.		4	25		
		1 pc. Rope 1", 250 ft.		12	50		
		1 pc. Rope 1", 145 ft.		7	25		
		2 – Spud Wrenches	@ .25		50		
		2 – Steel Clamps	@ 1.00	2	00		
		5 – Socket Wrenches	@ .50	2	50		
		7 – Blacksmith Tongs	@ 1.50	10	50		
		45 – Drift Pins	@ .10	4	50		
		1 – Ratch Wrench		2	50		
		3 – Grates	@ 1.50	4	50		
		1 – Straight Edge		1	25		
		18 ft. Wire Screen)					
		15 ft. #8 Wire Screen)					
		10 ft. #12 Fine Screen)– – – –		2	00		
		10 ft. #14 Fine Screen)					
		Carried Forward		$1,900	28		

THE HUTTER CONSTRUCTION CO.
BUILDERS
136 WESTERN AVENUE
PHONE 712
FOND DU LAC, WISCONSIN

DATE Aug.18, 1936

TERMS Net

CONST. NO 3625

SOLD TO   St. Peter's Cathedral

Marquette, Michigan

INVOICE NO. 1131

CAR NO. CGW 43162

RETAIN THIS BILL AS IT IS THE ONLY ITEMIZED BILL YOU WILL RECEIVE. IF NOT CORRECT PLEASE NOTIFY US AT ONCE   Page 6.

REG. NO.	DAY	ITEMS	CHARGES		CREDITS		BALANCE
		Brought Forward	$1,900	28			
		See Page 1-Item of 60-3/8" Cable Clips @ .36					
		amount extended in error 19.60					
		corrected amount 21.60	2	00			
		See Page 2-Item of 4 pcs. 6x8-10 Timbers 160 ft.)					
		4 " 8x8-10 " 213 ")					
		373 ft.@$25					
		amount extended in error 9.42					
		corrected amount 9.32				10	
		Item of 5 - Scoops #3 @ 1.35					
		amount extended in error 6.85					
		corrected amount 6.75				10	
		See Page 3-Item of 6 pcs. Chain - heavy - 98 ft.@ .20					
		amount extended in error 19.80					
		corrected amount 19.60				20	
		Item of 1 - 5 gal. Can IsoVis #30 @ .55					
		amount extended in error 3.30					
		corrected amount 2.75				55	
		Item of 6 - Points @ 2.25					
		amount extended in error 13.25					
		corrected amount 13.50		25			
			1,902	53		95	
				95			
		Total	$1,901	58			

446

TABLE IV

SUMMARY OF INVOICES RENDERED

FROM

THE HUTTER CONSTRUCTION COMPANY

Form No. 111 2M-8-36

THE HUTTER CONSTRUCTION CO.

BUILDERS

134 WESTERN AVENUE
PHONE 900
FOND DU LAC, WISCONSIN

DATE   December 15, 1937

TERMS

INVOICE NO.   3625

SOLD TO

Very Rev. Msgr. H. A. Buchholtz
Saint Peter's Cathedral
Marquette, Michigan

In re: St. Peter's Cathedral

Retain this Bill as it is the Only Itemized Bill You Will Receive. If Not Correct Notify Us At Once.

SUMMARY OF INVOICES RENDERED

REG. NO.		DAY	ITEMS		Net Cost	*CHARGES* Service Fee		*CREDITS* Total Cost	
1936	Aug.	31	Estimate	# 1	$ 10,144.90	963	77	11,108	77
	Sept	15	"	# 2	6,545.09	621	78	7,166	87
		30	"	# 3	12,796.87	1,215	70	14,012	57
	Oct.	15	"	# 4	16,589.68	1,576	02	18,165	70
		31	"	# 5	25,434.62	2,416	29	27,850	91
	Nov.	14	"	# 6	14,349.59	1,363	21	15,712	80
		30	"	# 7	6,081.19	577	71	6,658	90
		30	"	# 7A	2,859.46	271	65	3,131	11
	Dec.	15	"	# 8	9,690.39	925	34	10,615	73
		31	"	# 9	6,987.07	654	27	7,641	34
1937	Jan.	15	"	#10	5,880.71	558	67	6,439	38
	Feb.	1	"	#11	9,610.02	912	95	10,522	97
		15	"	#12	2,744.33	260	71	3,005	04
	Mar.	1	"	#13	3,253.68	309	10	3,562	78
		15	"	#14	8,239.62	782	76	9,022	38
		31	"	#15	9,421.70	895	06	10,316	76
	Apr.	15	"	#16	13,124.29	1,246	81	14,371	10
		30	"	#17	8,964.90	854	78	9,819	68
	May	15	"	#18	5,789.17	549	97	6,339	14
		29	"	#19	5,430.48	515	90	5,946	38
	June	15	"	#20	5,459.74	518	68	5,978	42
		30	"	#21	2,156.30	204	85	2,361	15
	July	15	"	#22	4,984.78	473	55	5,458	33
	Aug.	2	"	#23	870.84	88	25	959	09
		16	"	#24	4,650.13	441	76	5,091	89
	Sept	4	"	#25	3,586.91	340	76	3,927	67
		29	"	#26	368.38	35	00	403	38
	Oct.	1	"	#27	1,808.52	171	81	1,980	33
		20	"	#28	3,461.35	328	83	3,790	18
	Nov.	15	"	#29	6,128.50	Cr. 75	94	6,052	56
		26	"	#30	Cr. 13.20			Cr. 13	20
	Dec.	15	"	#31	Cr. 490.61			Cr. 490	61
	Nov.	26	Credit memo		Cr. 48.00			Cr. 48	00
			Totals		$216,861.40	$20,000	00	$236,861	40

TABLE V

STATEMENT OF ACCOUNT

FROM

THE HUTTER CONSTRUCTION COMPANY

THE HUTTER CONSTRUCTION CO.
BUILDERS
134 WESTERN AVENUE
PHONE 900
FOND DU LAC, WISCONSIN

DATE Dec. 15, 1937.

TERMS

INVOICE NO.

SOLD TO Very Rev. Msgr. H. A. Buchholtz,
Saint Peter's Cathedral,
Marquette, Michigan.

In re: St. Peter's Cathedral.

Retain this Bill as it is the Only Itemized Bill You Will Receive. If Not Correct Notify Us At Once.

REG. NO.	DAY	ITEMS		CHARGES		CREDITS
		Statement of Account.				
Dec.	15	Summary of Invoice #1 to 31 – per statement	$	236,861	40	
Nov.	16	Invoice rendered – Service fee on extras		1,059	63	
Nov.	16	Invoice rendered – Service fee on extras		1,919	88	
Dec.	15	Invoice rendered – Our share of savings		7,705	12	
		Total – Job No. 3625.	$	247,546	03	
Nov.	26	Credit by Payments made per statement rendered		245,186	76	
		Balance due on Job No. 3625	$	2,359	27	
Oct.	4	To invoice rendered – Alcott Playgrounds – Lumber, etc.		205	62	
Aug.	16	To invoice rendered – Material for Baraga High School		195	60	
			$	2,760	49	
Nov.	23	To invoice rendered – No. 2-3721		278	87	
		Total	$	3,039	36	
July	15	To invoice rendered – No. 1-3707	$ 2,185.05			
Oct.	19	To invoice rendered – No. 2-3707	1,646.13			
Nov.	23	To invoice rendered – No. 3-3707	291.63			
Dec.	15	To invoice rendered – No. 4-3707	137.13			
		Total invoices on Job No. 3707		4,259	94	
Dec.	15	Total balance due	$	7,299	30	

TABLE VI

RECAPITULATION AND ANALYSIS OF SAVINGS

FROM

THE HUTTER CONSTRUCTION COMPANY

THE HUTTER CONSTRUCTION CO.
BUILDERS

134 WESTERN AVENUE
PHONE 900
FOND DU LAC, WISCONSIN

DATE December 15, 1937

TERMS Regular

INVOICE NO. Job 3625

SOLD TO St. Peter's Cathedral,
Marquette, Michigan

RECAPITULATION AND ANALYSIS OF SAVINGS:

Retain this Bill as it is the Only Itemized Bill You Will Receive. If Not Correct Notify Us At Once.

REG. NO.	DAY	ITEMS	CHARGES	CREDITS
		Limit of Cost per contract, including Service Fee of $20,000.00	231,000.00	
		Credits to Limit of Cost due to changes and omissions (Detailed statement attached)		962.13
		Additions to Limit of Cost due to Changes and Additions:		
		Changes and Extras to Contract covered by signed orders (Detailed statements furnished), including Service Charge	18,888.40	
		Changes and Extras to Contract not covered by signed orders but authorized or ordered by Mr. Edward A. Schilling, Architect, Mr. Grimme, Architect's Superintendent, or by the Owners (Detailed statements furnished), including Service Charge.	11,324.89	
			$ 261,213.29	962.13
		NEW LIMIT OF COST	$ 260,251.16	
		Total Cost of all work (both contract and Extra), including Service Charge on Contract and Service Charge on Changes and Extras (Detail attached)	239,840.91	
		TOTAL SAVING EFFECTED	$ 20,410.25	
		The first $5,000.00 of Savings to the Owners	5,000.00	
		Balance of Savings to be divided equally between the Owner and the Contractor	15,410.25	
		Contractor's Share of Savings	$ 7,705.12	
		(Owner's Share of Savings--$12,705.13)		

THE HUTTER CONSTRUCTION CO.
BUILDERS
134 WESTERN AVENUE
PHONE 900
FOND DU LAC, WISCONSIN

DATE December 15, 1937

TERMS   Regular

INVOICE NO. Job 3625

OLD TO St. Peter's Cathedral,
Marquette, Michigan

RECAPITULATION AND ANALYSIS OF SAVINGS:

Retain this Bill as it is the Only Itemized Bill You Will Receive. If Not Correct Notify Us At Once.

REG. NO.	DAY	ITEMS	CHARGES	CREDITS
		Limit of Cost per contract, including Service Fee of $20,000.00	231,000.00	
		Credits to Limit of Cost due to changes and omissions (Detailed statement attached)		962.13
		Additions to Limit of Cost due to Changes and Additions:		
		Changes and Extras to Contract covered by signed orders (Detailed statements furnished), including Service Charge	18,888.40	
		Changes and Extras to Contract not covered by signed orders but authorized or ordered by Mr. Edward A. Schilling, Architect, Mr. Grimme, Architect's Superintendent, or by the Owners (Detailed statements furnished), including Service Charge.	11,324.89	
			$ 261,213.29	962.13
		NEW LIMIT OF COST	$ 260,251.16	
		Total Cost of all work (both contract and Extra), including Service Charge on Contract and Service Charge on Changes and Extras (Detail attached)	239,840.91	
		TOTAL SAVING EFFECTED	$ 20,410.25	
		The first $5,000.00 of Savings to the Owners	5,000.00	
		Balance of Savings to be divided equally between the Owner and the Contractor	15,410.25	
		Contractor's Share of Savings	$ 7,705.12	
		(Owner's Share of Savings--$12,705.13)		

TABLE VII

CHARGES AND APPROVED EXTRAS

FROM

THE HUTTER CONSTRUCTION COMPANY

THE HUTTER CONSTRUCTION CO.
BUILDERS
134 WESTERN AVENUE
PHONE 900
FOND DU LAC, WISCONSIN

DATE Nov. 5, 1937

TERMS Regular

INVOICE NO. 3625

SOLD TO St. Peter's Cathedral

Marquette, Michigan

CHANGES AND EXTRAS COVERED BY SIGNED ORDERS!
Retain this Bill as it is the Only Itemized Bill You Will Receive. If Not Correct Notify Us At Once.

REG. NO.	DAY	ITEMS	CHARGES		CREDITS
		Additions to the Limit of Cost of our Contract as evidenced by the following Change Orders:--			
Aug. 1	'36	Changing exterior construction of two main towers and the small tower in accordance with instructions from Mr. Edward A. Schilling in letter of July 27, 1936.	$ 2,300	00	
Sept. 11,		Change in steel sash and ventilators.	774	00	
Nov. 3,	'36	Changing floors from Gibraltar to terrazzo in accordance with our letter of October 1, 1936.	1,749	88	
		Furnishing terrazzo in Community Room in lieu of Gibraltar floors and wood steps and platform.	980	00	
		Furnishing terrazzo in lieu of linoleum where linoleum was specified.	111	00	
		Furnishing iron grills.	393	92	
		Change in balcony construction.	274	00	
		Furnishing additional I-beams and change in bar joist construction necessary to support steps of balcony.	145	44	
		Revision to Stair No. 1.	995	79	
		Glazed Brictile in Community Room	1,235	00	
		Vitritile wainscotting in kitchen.	390	00	
		Vitritile in toilet rooms.	190	00	
		Bufftone Brictile in lieu of gray brick where brick was specified.	450	00	
Nov. 30	'36	Furnishing metal lath, plaster and accoustical plaster to ceiling in Community Room	196	75	
Dec. 21	'36	Changing floors in Sacristy the passageway over ambulatory and the balcony of the bishop's chapel to cement construc-	374	42	

THE HUTTER CONSTRUCTION CO.
BUILDERS

134 WESTERN AVENUE
PHONE 900
FOND DU LAC, WISCONSIN

DATE Nov. 5, 1937

TERMS Regular

SOLD TO St. Peter's Cathedral

Marquette, Michigan

INVOICE NO. 3625

Retain this Bill as it is the Only Itemized Bill You Will Receive. If Not Correct Notify Us At Once.

REG. NO.	DAY	ITEMS —Page 2—	CHARGES		CREDITS
		tion with finish floor of asphalt tile.			
Jan. 9	'37	Changes in sanctuary arcades; terra cotta for frames; steel for lintel construction	1,400	00	
		Steel sash extensions (Drawing #139)	700	00	
Jun.29	'37	Furring ceiling arches and providing panel backing for accoustical tile.	1,191	60	
		Change in tile work; Addition due to furnishing tile work in accordance with Martin-Gibson Company's proposal.	1,679	72	
Feb.12	'37	Insulating ceiling with Sprayo-Flake	2,160	00	
Apr.17	'37	Altar curb rail.	535	68	
Apr.19	'37	Changing chapel communion rail.	519	20	
Apr.25	'37	Changing confessional floors from wood to asphalt tile.	142	00	
			$18,888	40	

THE HUTTER CONSTRUCTION CO.

BUILDERS

134 WESTERN AVENUE
PHONE 900
FOND DU LAC, WISCONSIN

DATE Nov. 16, 1937

TERMS Regular

INVOICE NO. 3625

SOLD TO St. Peter's Cathedral
Marquette, Michigan

Retain this Bill as it is the Only Itemized Bill You Will Receive. If Not Correct Notify Us At Once.

REG. NO.	DAY	ITEMS	CHARGES		CREDITS
		SERVICE CHARGE on extras and changes not covered by signed orders.			
		Extra No. 1: Removing Bishop's Bodies from crypt to passage to rectory and bricking up passage 31.80	3	66	
		Extra No. 2: Changing door from stair hall to chapel vestibule which was set wrong, due to a discrepancy in Architect's detail 10.18	1	17	
		Extra No. 4: Cutting holes in walls in confessionals so that radiators would fit 21.09	2	43	
		Extra No. 5: Cutting openings in old front wall at narthex for heat ducts 31.32	3	60	
		Extra No. 6: Bases for radiators in shrine at confessionals (Ordered by Mr. Grimme) 6.31		73	
		Extra No. 7: Insulating radiators at top of confessionals (Ordered by Mr. Grimme) 6.92		80	
		Extra No. 8: Installing additional slabs in crypt 222.69	25	62	
		Extra No. 9: Moving window over door to entrance at Stair hall #2 46.17	5	31	
		Extra No.10: Raising the level of the floor in the chapel 154.76	17	80	
		Extra No.12: Installing lath at light trough according to Architect's Detail #161 3.51		40	

Form No. 111 2M-8-36

THE HUTTER CONSTRUCTION CO.

BUILDERS

134 WESTERN AVENUE
PHONE 900
FOND DU LAC, WISCONSIN

DATE Nov. 16, 1937

TERMS Regular

INVOICE NO. 3625

SOLD TO St. Peter's Cathedral

Marquette, Michigan

Page 2 - Revised

Retain this Bill as it is the Only Itemized Bill You Will Receive. If Not Correct Notify Us At Once.

REG. NO.	DAY	ITEMS		CHARGES	CREDITS
		Extra No. 13:	Changing the access openings at the blind window in the chapel organ loft	16.28	1.87
		Extra No. 14:	Cutting openings for four stations	9.59	1.10
		Extra No. 15:	Cutting chase for flashing on roof over Sacristy #1	45.80	5.27
		Extra No. 16:	Cutting, bricking up and plastering recesses in front wall of nave at both sides of main sanctuary for the side altars	22.32	2.57
		Extra No. 17:	Cutting stone on towers for the setting of terra cotta grilles	341.09	39.24
		Extra No. 18:	Changing openings in the sanctuary at the ambulatory	14.57	1.68
		Extra No. 19:	Cutting buttress caps	385.05	44.30
		Extra No. 20:	Painting backs of the radiator recesses	18.05	2.08
		Extra No. 21:	Foundation walls and slab for north entrance steps and foundation walls for east entrance	418.95	48.20
		Extra No. 22:	Rebuilding wing walls at north and east and north entrance steps	204.71	23.55
		Extra No. 23:	Have increased the height of organ chamber 12'	111.53	12.74

THE HUTTER CONSTRUCTION CO.

BUILDERS

134 WESTERN AVENUE
PHONE 900
FOND DU LAC, WISCONSIN

DATE Nov. 15, 1937

TERMS Regular

INVOICE NO. 3625

SOLD TO St. Peter's Cathedral

Marquette, Michigan

Retain this Bill as it is the Only Itemized Bill You Will Receive. If Not Correct Notify Us At Once.

REG. NO.	DAY	ITEMS	CHARGES		CREDITS
		Page 3			
		Extra No. 24: Cutting a recess for drinking fountain in first floor of east tower due to changes in location of fountain 59.22	6	81	
		Extra No. 25: Raising bells in each tower 170.62	19	63	
		Extra No. 26: Installing lattice work in opening in west tower at organ chamber 80.32	7	99	
		Extra No. 27: Erecting and dismantling scaffold for interior decoration 175.83	20	23	
		Extra No.27A: Removing scaffold used for decorating chapel (This scaffold was erected by Mr. Grimme) 85.27	9	81	
		Extra No. 28: Raising scaffold to paint the cornice 103.61	11	92	
		Extra No. 30: Replacing sidewalks on north and east sides of cathedral 567.61	65	30	
		Extra No. 31: Trimming belt course on the towers located two courses above the water table __.58	__	60	
		Extra No. 32: Replacing iron railings on each entrance stairway 16.79	1	93	
		Extra No. 33: Repairing retaining wall at the west property line of the cathedral 3_.18	4	05	
		Extra No. 35: Cleaning up basement due to heavy rains 54.05	6	22	
		Extra No. 36: Closing window opening between sacristy and chapel _7.65		88	

Form No. 111 2M-8-35

The Hutter Construction Co.
BUILDERS
134 WESTERN AVENUE
PHONE 900
FOND DU LAC, WISCONSIN

DATE Nov. 16, 1937

TERMS Regular

INVOICE NO. 3625

SOLD TO St. Peter's Cathedral

Marquette, Michigan

Retain this Bill as it is the Only Itemized Bill You Will Receive. If Not Correct Notify Us At Once.

REG. NO.	DAY	Page 4 — ITEMS		CHARGES		CREDITS
		Extra No. 38: Placing rubber bumpers on door stops	61.97	7	13	
		Extra No. 39: Applying card holders	15.58	1	79	
		Extra No. 40: Placing an extra lock in organ chamber; cutting and fitting celotex in altar background; miscellaneous odd jobs in connection with placing altars, etc.	25.24	2	90	
		Extra No. 41: Cleaning, dusting and helping on organ; miscellaneous work in connection with moving into upper church	30.81	3	54	
		Extra No.41A: Moving temporary fixtures in basement used for church purposes	21.11	2	43	
		Extra No.41B: Cleaning basement and temporary arrangements for sales room for Mission goods	6.52		75	
		Extra No.41C: Placing towel bars, soap dishes and extra shelving in south partition in drawers of Vestment Case in Sacristy #2	4.61		53	
		Extra No.41D: Placing three mortised bolts in three toilet doors	4.63		53	
		Scrubbing and cleaning chapel	41.46	4	77	
		Temporary back-ground for altars--main sanctuary	7.59		87	
		Platform in organ loft for the Director of Music	16.78	1	93	
		Pointing church rectory	38.83	4	47	

THE HUTTER CONSTRUCTION CO.
BUILDERS
134 WESTERN AVENUE
PHONE 900
FOND DU LAC, WISCONSIN

DATE Nov. 10, 1937

TERMS Regular

INVOICE NO. 3625

SOLD TO St. Peter's Cathedral

Marquette, Michigan

Retain this Bill as it is the Only Itemized Bill You Will Receive. If Not Correct Notify Us At Once.

REG. NO.	DAY	ITEMS	CHARGES		CREDITS
		Page 5			
		Preparation of basement for temporary use	163.60	18 82	
		Cutting chase in floor and wall of machinery room for steam pipe returns (Ordered by Mr. Grimme)	10.40	1 20	
		Extra electrical work in school (Ordered by Mr. Grimme)	23.50	1 74	
		Extra work on school building (Ordered by Mr. Grimme)	7.50	56	
		Extra excavation for machinery room; extra excavation for the organ machinery room	105.90	12 19	
		Trimming masonry in tower to accommodate Stair "A"	112.40	7 30	
		Cutting opening for organ machinery room	35.80	3 67	
		Cutting opening for machinery room to accommodate return pipes, etc.	20.00	2 08	
		Concrete piers and lintels for confessional doors at the east and west side confessionals	70.90	8 16	
		Furring out main altar	158.70	18 26	
		Use of precast imitation Kechu stone materials for all wainscoting, which were originally to be plastered	1000.00	80 00	
		Increasing height of the wainscoting in the shrines at the confessional	43.20	3 20	

THE HUTTER CONSTRUCTION CO.
BUILDERS
134 WESTERN AVENUE
PHONE 900
FOND DU LAC, WISCONSIN

DATE Nov. 16, 1937

TERMS Regular

INVOICE NO. 3625

SOLD TO St. Peter's Cathedral

Marquette, Michigan

Page 6 - Revised

Retain this Bill as it is the Only Itemized Bill You Will Receive. If Not Correct Notify Us At Once.

REG. NO.	DAY	ITEMS	CHARGES	CREDITS
		Door and frame from Community Room to present west tunnel for which no new door was scheduled	92.24	10.61
		Rollers for vestment cases	104.76	7.76
		Channel iron door frame for exterior "B" type door	54.00	4.00
		Miscellaneous changes in roofing and sheet metal work	458.38	33.95
		Changes in Sanctuary as listed	386.11	44.42
		General changes in sanctuary and chapel	1,386.93	102.74
		Temporary back-ground for altars--main sanctuary	21.54	1.90
		Screens and screen hardware for five screens in kitchen and storage pantry	53.13	6.11
		Changes to crosses and finials	261.52	19.37
		Brass thresholds at five exterior doors	95.07	10.94
		Additional cost of finish hardware	443.47	32.85
		Additional steel ladder in east tower	34.00	3.91
		Imitation Mankato stone for arches-- entrance to crypt	92.88	6.88
		Lathing and plastering stair soffits-- Stairs Nos. 1-2-3	72.55	8.35
		Steel sash for two main towers	601.80	47.55

THE HUTTER CONSTRUCTION CO.
BUILDERS
134 WESTERN AVENUE
PHONE 900
FOND DU LAC, WISCONSIN

DATE Nov. 16, 1937

TERMS Regular

INVOICE NO. 3625

SOLD TO St. Peter's Cathedral

Marquette, Michigan

Page 7 - Revised

Retain this Bill as it is the Only Itemized Bill You Will Receive. If Not Correct Notify Us At Once.

REG. NO.	DAY	ITEMS	CHARGES	CREDITS
		Bronzing door checks in main vestibule to match balance of hardware	21.98	1.63
		Re-painting radiator grilles	36.71	2.72
		General changes in sanctuary and chapel	307.45	35.37
		Change in 9 casement projected sash	72.53	5.37
		Extra terrazzo work	921.05	68.23
		Changing toilet partitions in basement toilets from wood to metal	61.88	4.58
		Extra on interior painting	136.08	10.08
			$ 11,324.89	$ 1,059.63

Service Fee on Extras not covered by

Signed Orders !

TABLE IX

DETAILED ESTIMATE

FOR PLUMBING AND HEATING

FROM

LEVINE BROTHERS

August 1, 1936

DETAILED ESTIMATE---------------PLUMBING & HEATING

Item No.		Material Cost Dollars	Labor cost Dollars	Total cost Dollars
	HEATING			
1.	Removing Boilers & Cleaning Boiler Room		245.00	245.00
2.	Rio-Wil	1,839.00	310.00	2,149.00
3.	Boilers	2,991.00	280.00	3,271.00
4.	Stokers	1,949.00	400.00	2,349.00
5.	Boiler Headers (Steam & Return) & Trimmings	730.00	250.00	980.00
6.	Condensation Pump	356.00	124.00	480.00
7.	Ash Hoist	98.00	80.00	178.00
8.	Fan Equipment	521.00	380.00	901.00
9.	Vento Units Tempering & Re-heating Radiators	875.00	250.00	1,125.00
10.	Radiation	1,212.50	292.00	1,504.50
11.	Valves & Traps	240.00	60.00	300.00
12.	Breeching for Boilers	105.00	65.00	170.00
13.	Concrete Manholes	48.00	32.00	80.00
14.	Concrete Anchors on Main	31.00	29.00	60.00
15.	Concrete Foundation for Boilers & Stokers	36.00	42.00	78.00
16.	Concrete for Exhaust Fans & Duct	35.00	28.00	63.00
17.	6" Steam & 1½" Return Piping to Cathedral	682.00	185.00	867.00
18.	Steam Mains in Cathedral	604.50	320.00	924.50
19.	Steam Returns in Cathedral	228.00	190.00	418.00
20.	Risers to Radiation & Ventos	132.00	180.00	212.00
21.	Ventilating	1,953.00	862.00	2,815.00
22.	Covering Boilers & Breeching	363.00	160.00	523.00
23.	Pipe Covering in Boiler Room	58.00	38.00	96.00
24.	Covering in Cathedral	171.00	172.00	343.00
25.	Hangers & Sleeves			
26.	Venting for Vaults	118.00	82.00	200.00
	PLUMBING			
27.	Painting	35.00	120.00	155.00
28.	Sump Pump & Sump	138.00	42.00	180.00
29.	Plumbing Fixtures	430.00	52.00	482.00
30.	Sewer from Street to Building	48.00	72.00	120.00
31.	X.H. Soil Pipe beneath Basement Floor	178.00	52.00	230.00
32.	Soil Stacks & Fittings	170.00	30.00	200.00
33.	Water Pipe & Fittings	81.00	77.00	158.00
34.	Pipe Covering	38.88	20.00	58.88
		16,494.88	5,421.00	21,915.88

TABLE X

CONTRACT AGREEMENT

BETWEEN

THE HUTTER CONSTRUCTION COMPANY

AND

THE DIOCESE OF SAULT STE. MARIE & MARQUETTE

A FORM OF
AGREEMENT BETWEEN CONTRACTOR AND OWNER

ISSUED BY THE AMERICAN INSTITUTE OF ARCHITECTS FOR USE WHEN
THE COST OF THE WORK PLUS A FEE FORMS THE BASIS OF PAYMENT.

FOURTH EDITION—COPYRIGHT 1920–1925 BY THE AMERICAN INSTITUTE OF ARCHITECTS, WASHINGTON, D. C.

THIS FORM IS TO BE USED ONLY WITH THE INSTITUTE'S STANDARD GENERAL CONDITIONS OF THE CONTRACT, FOURTH EDITION, 1925, AND IT SHOULD NOT BE USED WITHOUT CAREFUL STUDY OF ITS ACCOMPANYING "CIRCULAR OF INFORMATION."

THIS AGREEMENT made the ...twenty-fourth...

day of.....July.....in the year nineteen hundred and...thirty-six

by and between...Hutter Construction Company, Fond du Lac, Wisconsin, a Wisconsin corporation, liscensed to do business in the State of Michigan,

hereinafter called the Contractor, and.... Most Reverend Joseph C. Plagens, Bishop of the Diocese, _(AS ROMAN CATHOLIC) (OF SAULT STE MARIE AND)_ Marquette, Michigan,

.....hereinafter called the Owner,

WITNESSETH, that whereas the Owner intends to erect.....Additions and Alterations to St. Peter's Cathedral, Marquette, Michigan.

NOW, THEREFORE, the Contractor and the Owner, for the considerations hereinafter named, agree as follows:

Article 1. The Work to be Done and the Documents Forming the Contract.

The Contractor agrees to provide all the labor and materials and to do all things necessary for the proper construction and completion of the work shown and described on Drawings bearing the title.....

and numbered.....

and in Specifications bearing the same title, the pages of which are numbered..........

The said Drawings and Specifications and the General Conditions of the Contract

ARTICLE I.   The Work to be Done and the Documents Forming
the Contract.

The Contractor agrees to provide all labor and materials
and do all things necessary for the proper construction and completion of the work shown and described on the following drawings and specifications, which drawings and specifications and
the General Conditions of the Contract (Standard Form of The American Institute of Architects-Fourth Edition) constitute the
contract.

<u>DRAWINGS</u>

<u>Architectural Drawings</u>

#1 - dated June 27, 1936	- Plot Plan-Room Finish Schedule
#A2- " " " (Dim. Revised 7/1/36 (G.E.G.)	- Basement Plan
#A3- dated June 27, 1936 (Dim. Revised 7/1/36 (G.E.G.)	- First Floor Plan
#A4- dated June 27, 1936 (Dim. Revised 7/1/36 (G.E.G.)	- Clerestory Plan
#A5- (dated June 27, 1936 (Revised 7/2/36	- Additional plank walk added; roof plan details; Section DD; CC; AA; EE; BB; FF.
#A6- dated June 27, 1936	- Front and rear elevations Note: All dotted stone indicates Ohio Sand Stone
#A7- dated June 27, 1936	- Side elevation (east) Note: All dotted stone indicates Ohio Sand Stone
#A8- dated June 27, 1936	- Side elevation (west)
#A9- dated June 27, 1936	- Exterior scale details Note: All dotted stone indicates Ohio Sand Stone
#A10-dated June 27, 1936	- Longitudinal section
#A11- " " "	- Interior scale details
#A12- " " "	- Interior chapel details
#A13 " " "	- Details for confessionals, shrine and pulpit
#A14 " " "	- Narthex details
#A15 " " "	- Stair details
#A16 " " "	- Miscellaneous details
#A17 " " "	- Miscellaneous details
#A20 " " "	- Present north and south elevations

ARTICLE I.   Continued

The Drawings and Specifications were carefully analyzed in conferences on July 22, 1936 and July 24, 1936, between Mr. Edward A. Schilling, Architect, Mr. T. O. Pechauer, Chairman of the Building Committee, and Mr. George F. Hutter, of the Hutter Construction Company.

The following clarifications have been made and are to be considered as being corrections to the Specifications. The items hereinafter listed are to take precedence over the original phraseology of the Specifications and the Limit of Cost hereinafter referred to has been based upon the interpretations here listed:

Page 6 - <u>Temporary Heating</u>

It is understood that the Contractor will furnish all fuel, equipment, appurtenances, and labor, required for heating materials and affording such protection as may be required up to a point where the building is temporarily enclosed. The cost of this item of heating is included in the Contractor's Limit of Cost.

The Contractor will make every effort to give the Owner the occupancy of the basement for services at the earliest possible date and is hopeful of accomplishing this not later than December 25, 1936.

The Contractor does not include in his Limit of Cost the item of fuel for the temporary heating of the building until taken over by the Owner, but agrees to furnish the required labor for both day and night firing during the time that temporary heating is required. The cost of this labor will be a part of the cost of the work.

<u>Temporary Lighting and Power</u>

It is understood that any of the Mechanical Trades who have a separate contract with the Owner will pay for any electrical energy, temporary wiring, sockets, globes, service, etc., that they may ask the General Contractor to arrange for.

Page 8 - <u>Additions and Alterations to existing building</u>

Since the Owners are required to furnish the necessary brown stone to complete the work and because the brown stone on the premises make it impossible to conform the new masonry with the present masonry, it is understood that the additions and alterations indicated new on the drawings on the rear portions, including the Chapel and Sanctuary are to be laid up in what is known as "rubble ashlar". The general character and appearance of the work is to conform with that used on the First Baptist Church, in Marquette, Michigan.

ARTICLE I.   Continued

The Drawings and Specifications were carefully analyzed
in conferences on July 22, 1936 and July 24, 1936, between Mr.
Edward A. Schilling, Architect, Mr. T. O. Pechauer, Chairman
of the Building Committee, and Mr. George F. Hutter, of the
Hutter Construction Company.

The following clarifications have been made and are to be
considered as being corrections to the Specifications. The items
hereinafter listed are to take precedence over the original phraseology of the Specifications and the Limit of Cost hereinafter referred to has been based upon the interpretations here listed:

Page 6 - <u>Temporary Heating</u>

It is understood that the Contractor will furnish
all fuel, equipment, appurtenances, and labor, required for heating materials and affording such protection as may be required up
to a point where the building is temporarily enclosed. The cost
of this item of heating is included in the Contractor's Limit of
Cost.

The Contractor will make every effort to give the Owner the
occupancy of the basement for services at the earliest possible
date and is hopeful of accomplishing this not later than December
25, 1936.

The Contractor does not include in his Limit of Cost the
item of fuel for the temporary heating of the building until tak-
en over by the Owner, but agrees to furnish the required labor for
both day and night firing during the time that temporary heating is
required. The cost of this labor will be a part of the cost of the
work.

<u>Temporary Lighting and Power</u>

It is understood that any of the Mechanical Trades who have
a separate contract with the Owner will pay for any electrical
energy, temporary wiring, sockets, globes, service, etc., that
they may ask the General Contractor to arrange for.

Page 8 - <u>Additions and Alterations to existing building</u>

Since the Owners are required to furnish the necessary brown stone to complete the work and because the brown stone
on the premises make it impossible to conform the new masonry with
the present masonry, it is understood that the additions and alterations indicated new on the drawings on the rear portions, including the Chapel and Sanctuary are to be laid up in what is known as
"rubble ashlar". The general character and appearance of the work
is to conform with that used on the First Baptist Church, in Marquette, Michigan.

ARTICLE I.   Continued.

Page 11 - <u>Contractors' Responsibility</u>

It is to be distinctly understood that this Contractor does not assume the responsibility for the structural strength or the structural design of the entire building. It is understood, however, that this Contractor assumes the responsibility for any concrete, either plain or reinforced that may be incorporated in the work.

Page 14 - <u>Tests</u>

It is understood that certified mill tests for structural steel, reinforcing steel and Portland cement will be acceptable.

Page 22 - It is understood that the Contractor may use a structural building tile, known in the trade as a "Heath Cube", or its equal in lieu of the Denison Inter-locking tile specified, which does not lend itself to the type of backing intended.

Page 24 - It is understood that the Contractor has the option of using a steam wash process, if it is found that the nature of the stone will lend itself best to this type of washing in lieu of sand-blasting.

Page 27 - It is understood that the Owners have furnished and delivered to the site, or will furnish, all brown stone required for the exterior. In detailing the quantities of backing that will be required, the Contractor has based his cost upon all brown stone facing having a displacement in the wall of 8" in thickness. In the event that the brown stone will not work to this 8" displacement, any additional materials required will be figured at the following unit prices:

         Common brick backing   -   66¢ per cubic foot
         Hollow tile backing   -   40¢   "   "   "

In determining the estimate for the Limit of Cost, the Contractor is assuming that the work in connection with the brown stone exterior now standing has been completed and is taking the building in its present condition for completion.

It is understood that the Contractor will have the use of all lumber and scaffolding now on the premises.

Page 29 - <u>Ohio and Miscellaneous Stone</u>

To clarify the specifications, since there is no stone available known as Bedford Ohio Gray Sand Stone, the estimate is based upon using Bedford Indiana Gray Limestone stock.

<u>Main Window</u>

The stone work of the main window shall be of

ARTICLE I.   Continued.

Bedford Stone, as detailed, in lieu of Ohio Sand Stone.

Page 52 - <u>Carpentry</u>

It is understood that commercial sizes of
lumber are acceptable and that where oak nailers are specified, the same grade of Yellow Pine as specified for roof
framing generally will be acceptable.

Page 56 - <u>Composition Ornament</u>

Since the details and the information on the
drawings do not clearly indicate the intent or the amount of
composition ornamentation, this item is not included in the
mill figure nor the Limit of Cost and is assumed to be included in the details of the interior furniture and fixtures.

Pages 59 to 62 inclusive - <u>Painting</u>

It is understood that the painting specif-
ications do not contemplate any decorating or decorative painting features that may be shown on the drawings.
It is further understood that all interior decorating and decorations will be executed under a separate contract at a later date.

Page 63 - <u>Glass and Glazing</u>

Under the description of glass, it is understood that only the glass known as storm glass is included,
set in sash, and that the "leaded in panes" feature is not contemplated by this contract.

Pages 37 to 39 inclusive; Pages 39A and 69A - <u>Miscellaneous
Iron Work</u>

Because the drawings and specifications do not
indicate the thickness of metal required for various ornamental
iron guards and ornamental iron railings and not knowing what
was designated in the miscellaneous iron work specification of
Section D, the Contractor is herewith listing the figure used
in the preparation of our Limit of Cost figure and is enumerat-
ing the items which are based upon standard practise. In the
event that the ornamental iron details are elaborated upon, any
increase in cost as the result of such elaboration will be subject to adjustment.
The figure used is listed herewith:

For the furnishing and installing of the miscellaneous iron work--
Section "D", consisting of the following items:

ARTICLE I.   Continued

          Area Railings
          Window Spandrels
          Radiator Grilles and Shields
          Iron Stairs and Railings
          Stairs in Boiler Room
          Trap Pit Covers
          Iron Ladders
          Main Entrance and Nartox Door Frames
          Metal Cabinet Doors
          Pipe Hand Rail
          Cross Supports
          Steel Door
          Ornamental Grilles, Gates and Railing
          Door Frame for Kalamein Door--Boiler Room
          Window Guards

The Contractor has based his estimate upon the value of the ornamental iron work, erected, at FOUR THOUSAND NINE HUNDRED EIGHTY-THREE AND NO/100 DOLLARS ($4983.00).

Work For Other Trades

It is understood that this Contractor contemplates having other contractors for heating, plumbing, ventilating and electrical work place their own sleeves and do their own lay-out work and assume responsibility for their own lay-outs.

consisting of Articles numbered one to..
together with this Agreement, constitute the Contract; the Drawings, Specifications
and General Conditions being as fully a part thereof and hereof as if hereto attached
or herein repeated.   If anything in the said General Conditions is inconsistent with
this Agreement, the Agreement shall govern.

The said documents have been prepared by..

....

therein and hereinafter called the Architect.

Article 2. Changes in the Work.

The Owner, through the Architect, may from time to time, by written instructions
or drawings issued to the Contractor, make changes in the above-named Drawings
and Specifications, issue additional instructions, require additional work or direct
the omission of work previously ordered, and the provisions of this contract shall
apply to all such changes, modifications and additions with the same effect as if they
were embodied in the original Drawings and Specifications.   Since the cost of all such
changes is to merge in the final cost of the work, Articles 15 and 16 of the General
Conditions of the Contract are annulled, unless elsewhere especially made applicable.

Article 3. The Contractor's Duties and Status.

The Contractor recognizes the relations of trust and confidence established
between him and the Owner by this Agreement.   He covenants with the Owner to
furnish his best skill and judgment and to cooperate with the Architect in forwarding
the interests of the Owner.   He agrees to furnish efficient business administration and
superintendence and to use every effort to keep upon the work at all times an adequate
supply of workmen and materials, and to secure its execution in the best and soundest
way and in the most expeditious and economical manner consistent with the interests
of the Owner.

Article 4. Fee for Services.

ARTICLE 4.   <u>FEE FOR SERVICES</u>

Contractor shall receive a fixed fee for his services for the work hereinbefore described of TWENTY THOUSAND
AND NO/100 DOLLARS ($20,000.00), which sum is included in the
Limit of Cost of TWO HUNDRED THIRTY-ONE THOUSAND AND NO/100
DOLLARS ($231,000.00). Fee shall be paid in proportion as
the work progresses on certification of the Architect. No
separate charge shall be made for rental of equipment except
as noted in Article 7, Paragraphs E and F.

<u>SAVINGS</u>: The first FIVE THOUSAND DOLLARS ($5,000.00) of any
savings shall accrue to the Owner. Any balance over this
amount shall be divided equally between the Owner and the Contractor.

the standard paid in the locality of the work except with prior consent of the Owner:

(*a*) All labor directly on the Contractor's pay roll.

(*b*) Salaries of Contractor's Employees stationed at the field office, in whatever capacity employed. Employees engaged, at shops or on the road, in expediting the production or transportation of material, shall be considered as stationed at the field office and their salaries paid for such part of their time as is employed on this work.

(*c*) The proportion of transportation, traveling and hotel expenses of the Contractor or of his officers or employees incurred in discharge of duties connected with this work.

(*d*) All expenses incurred for transportation to and from the work of the force required for its prosecution.

(*e*) Permit fees, royalties, damages for infringement of patents, and costs of defending suits therefor and for deposits lost for causes other than the Contractor's negligence.

(*f*) Losses and expenses, not compensated by insurance or otherwise, sustained by the Contractor in connection with the work, provided they have resulted from causes other than the fault or neglect of the Contractor. Such losses shall include settlements made with the written consent and approval of the Owner. No such losses and expenses shall be included in the cost of the work for the purpose of determining the Contractor's fee, but if, after a loss from fire, flood or similar cause not due to the fault or neglect of the Contractor, he be put in charge of reconstruction, he shall be paid for his services a fee proportionate to that named in Article 4 hereof.

(*g*) Minor expenses, such as telegrams, telephone service, expressage, and similar petty cash items.

(*h*) Cost of hand tools, not owned by the workmen, canvas and tarpaulins, consumed in the prosecution of the work, and depreciation on such tools, canvas and tarpaulins used but not consumed and which shall remain the property of the Contractor.

Article 6. Costs Not to be Reimbursed.

Reimbursement of expenses to the Contractor shall not include any of the following:

(*a*) Salary of the Contractor, if an individual, or salary of any member of the Contractor, if a firm, or salary of any officer of the Contractor, if a corporation.

(*b*) Salary of any person employed, during the execution of the work, in the main office or in any regularly established branch office of the Contractor.

(*c*) Overhead or general expenses of any kind, except as these may be expressly included in Article 5.

(*d*) Interest on capital employed either in plant or in expenditures on the work, except as may be expressly included in Article 5.

ARTICLE 6A--<u>LIMIT OF COST</u>

In determining the Limit of Cost, the following figures were used:

Proposal, dated July 16, 1936, for $ 221,830.00

Supplementary Proposal for the furnishing of
terra cotta in lieu of brown stone and lime
stone for the two main towers and the tower
on the side elevation above the cornice; the
furnishing of such Indiana Limestone as may
be required for cornice features, in lieu of
brown stone,   for   8,883.00

Allowance for contingencies in adjustment of
stone and terra cotta figures   285.00

LIMIT OF COST, including Service Fee $ 231,000.00

<u>EXTRAS</u>

Extra work will be performed if ordered by the Owner
on the basis of actual cost to the Contractor plus eight (8%)
percent fee, if done by sub-contractors, or plus thirteen (13%)
percent if done directly by the Contractor, such percentages to
include all Contractor's charges for overhead and profit.

Article 7. Costs to be Paid ~~Direct~~ by the Owner.

In addition to items of cost noted in Article 5 for which the Owner reimburses the Contractor, the Owner shall pay all costs as follows:

(*a*) Materials, supplies, equipment and transportation required for the proper execution of the work, which shall include all temporary structures and their maintenance; all such costs to be at rates not higher than the standard paid in the locality of the work except with prior consent of the Owner.

(*b*) The amounts of all separate contracts.

(*c*) Premiums on all bonds and insurance policies called for under Articles 27, 28, 29 and 30 of the General Conditions of the Contract.

(*d*) Rentals of all construction plant or parts thereof, whether rented from the Contractor or others, in accordance with rental agreements approved by the Architect. Transportation of said construction plant, costs of loading and unloading, cost of installation, dismantling and removal thereof and minor repairs and replacements during its use on the work,—all in accordance with the terms of the said rental agreements.

(e) Small tools and equipment not customarily furnished by workmen, rubber boots, water and steam piping, hose, water pails, barrels, tarpaulins, air hose, all of which shall be charged as at cost, if new, or at proper depreciation value, if used, on delivery to the work and credited on completion of the work at the same cost, less a fair amount of depreciation subject to the approval of t e Architect.

(f) Rental of equipment not ordinarily owned by a general contractor, such as steam shovels, pile drivers, motor trucks, and teams, shall be charged on a rental basis as agreed between Contractor and Architect, which rental shall not be greater than current charges in the industry.

(g) The cost of all contributions as assessed for Unemployment Insurance under the Federal Social Security Act and the cost of all contributions that may be assessed as the result of any Unemployment Insurance Law that may be passed in the State of Michigan during the life of this contract.

which have been paid with his own funds.

All portions of the work that the Contractor's organization has not been accustomed to perform or that the Owner may direct, shall be executed under separate contracts let by the Owner direct. In such cases either the Contractor shall ask for bids from contractors approved by the Architect and shall deliver such bids to him, or the Architect shall procure such bids himself, and in either case the Architect shall determine, with the advice of the Contractor and subject to the approval of the Owner, the award and amount of the accepted bid. The Owner shall contract for such work direct with such approved bidders in accordance with the terms of this agreement and the General Conditions of the Contract, which Conditions shall, for the purposes of such contracts, stand as printed or written and not be subject to the modifications set forth herein.

The Contractor, being fully responsible for the general management of the building operation, shall have full directing authority over the execution of the separate contracts.

The separate Contractors shall not only cooperate with each other, as provided in Article 35 of the General Conditions of the Contract, but they shall conform to all directions of the Contractor in regard to the progress of the work.

Article 11. Title to the Work.

The title of all work completed and in course of construction and of all materials on account of which any payment has been made, and materials to be paid for under Article 7, shall be in the Owner.

Article 12. Accounting, Inspection, Audit.

The Contractor shall check all material and labor entering into the work and shall keep such full and detailed accounts as may be necessary to proper financial management under this Agreement and the system shall be such as is satisfactory to the Architect or to an auditor appointed by the Owner. The Architect, the auditor and their timekeepers and clerks shall be afforded access to the work and to all the Contractor's books, records, correspondence, instructions, drawings, receipts, vouchers, memoranda, etc., relating to this contract, and the Contractor shall preserve all such records for a period of two years after the final payment hereunder.

Article 13. Applications for Payment and the 15th and 20th

The Contractor shall, between the first and seventh/of each month, deliver to the Architect a statement, sworn to if required, showing in detail and as completely as possible all moneys paid out by him on account of the cost of the work during the previous month for which he is to be reimbursed under Article 5 hereof, with original pay rolls for labor, checked and approved by a person satisfactory to the Architect, and all receipted bills.

He shall at the same time submit to the Architect a complete statement of all moneys properly due for materials or on account of separate contracts, or on account of his fee, or otherwise, which are to be paid direct by the Owner under Article 7 hereof.

The provisions of this Article supersede those of Article 24 of the General Conditions of the Contract.

Article 14. Certificates of Payment.

The Architect shall check the Contractor's statements of moneys due, called for in Article 13, and shall promptly issue certificates to the Owner for all such as he approves, which certificates shall be payable on issuance.

The provisions of this Article supersede the first paragraph of Article 25 of the General Conditions of the Contract.

Article 15. Disbursements.

Should the Contractor neglect or refuse to pay, within five days after it falls due any bill legitimately incurred by him hereunder (and for which he is to be reimbursed under Article 5) the Owner, after giving the Contractor twenty-four hours' written notice of his intention so to do, shall have the right to pay such bill directly, in which event such payment shall not, for the purpose either of reimbursement or of calculating the Contractor's fee, be included in the cost of the work.

Article 16. Termination of Contract.

(The provisions of this Article supersede all of Article 22 of the General Conditions of the Contract except the first sentence.)

If the Owner should terminate the contract under the first sentence of Article 22 of the General Conditions of the Contract, he shall reimburse the Contractor for the balance of all payments made by him under Article 5, plus a fee computed upon the cost of the work to date at the rate of percentage named in Article 4 hereof, or if the Contractor's fee be stated as a fixed sum, the Owner shall pay the Contractor such an amount as will increase the payments on account of his fee to a sum which bears the same ratio to the said fixed sum as the cost of the work at the time of termination bears to a reasonable estimated cost of the work completed, and the Owner shall also pay to the Contractor fair compensation, either by purchase or rental, at the election of the Owner, for any equipment retained.   In case of such termination of the contract the Owner shall further assume and become liable for all obligations, commitments and unliquidated claims that the Contractor may have theretofore, in good faith, undertaken or incurred in connection with said work and the Contractor shall, as a condition of receiving the payments mentioned in this Article, execute and deliver all such papers and take all such steps, including the legal assignment of his contractual rights, as the Owner may require for the purpose of fully vesting in him the rights and benefits of the Contractor under such obligations or commitments.

The Contractor and the Owner for themselves, their successors, executors, administrators and assigns hereby agree to the full performance of the covenants herein contained.

IN WITNESS WHEREOF they have executed this agreement the day and year first above written.

<u>COMPLETION</u>:

The work to be performed under this contract shall be commenced immediately after notification. The Contractor will make every effort to give the Owners occupancy of the basement for use by December 15, 1936. The entire work shall be completed within ten (10) months of the Owner's notification to begin work.

<u>GENERAL CONDITIONS</u>:

The Articles of the General Conditions of the Contract referred to in this Contract are the Standard Form of the General Conditions of the Contract, Fourth Edition, issued by the American Institute of Architects.

(Executed in quadruplicate, each of which is an original)

IN WITNESS WHEREOF the parties hereto have executed this Agreement, the day and year first above written.

In Presence of:

RUTTER CONSTRUCTION COMPANY

BY _______________________________
                        PRESIDENT

MOST REVEREND JOSEPH C. PLAGENS, BISHOP OF THE DIOCESE, Marquette, Michigan.

BY _______________________________
                        Pastor

TABLE XI

PAYROLL REPORT

FROM

THE HUTTER CONSTRUCTION COMPANY

Hutter Construction Company
Fond du Lac, Wisconsin

St. Peter's Cathedral
Marquette, Michigan

Payroll Report
Contract No. 3625
Week Ending 7/31/37

Employee Name	Occupation	Total Hours	Rate	Amount
C. A. Lymeis	Supt.	44	$15.00	$71.43
C. J. Brown		27	30.00	16.40
M. Redlin	Carp.	60	.90	54.00
F. Neuberger	H. M.	4	.90	3.60
M. Vatcher		4	.90	3.60
M. Lepan/A. Musoff	Labor	18	.60	10.80
C. Schrage/Syl. Guelig	Labor	36	.60	21.60
A. Hogan	Labor	2	.55	1.10
W. Cody	Labor	49	.45	22.05
T. Fennessy	Labor	21	.45	9.45
A. Grimsby	Labor	18	.45	8.10
J. Dunleavy	Labor	25	.45	11.25
G. Jahoubek				
P. Bennard				

TOTAL: $229.78

BIBLIOGRAPHY

[1] Rezek, Rev. Antoine, Ivan, History of The Diocese of Sault Ste. Marie and Marquette. Vol. I & II; M. A. Donahue & Co., Chicago, Houghton, Michigan, 1907.

[2] The Mining Journal; "St. Peter's Cathedral Twice Destroyed by Fire: Parish Formed Nearly Century Ago"; Marquette, Mich., pp. 9 & 14; Tuesday, May 10, 1949.

[3] Our Sunday Visitor, "St. Peter's Marquette, Founded 1853, by Mrs. Agnes Graham", Official Newspaper of the Diocese of Marquette; Vol. XLII, #18; August 30, 1953.

[4] Pechaeur, Anthony, Personal Communication.

[5] Cappo, Rev. Louis, C., Personal Communication.

[6] Press Release published by the Marquette Mining Journal, Marquette, Mich.; August, 1936.

[7] Personal Correspondence between Archie J. Verville, General Building Construction, Hancock, Michigan, and Monsignor H. A. Buchholtz, P.A., Rector, St. Peter's Cathedral, Marquette, Mich.; May 9, 1936.

[8] Contract between Archie J. Verville, General Building Construction and Monsignor H. A. Buchholtz, P.A., Rector, St. Peter's Cathedral; May 16, 1936.

[9] Personal Correspondence between Archie J. Verville, General Building Construction and Edward A. Schilling, Architect, 409 Griswold, Detroit, Mich., June 13, 1936.

[10] Personal Correspondence between Edward A. Schilling, Architect and Monsignor H. A. Buchholtz, P.A., Rector, St. Peter's Cathedral; June 26, 1936.

[11] Personal Correspondence between Edward A. Schilling, Architect and Monsignor H.A. BUchholtz, P.A., Rector, St. Peter's Cathedral; June 27, 1936.

[12] Personal Correspondence between Archie J. Verville, General Building Construction, and Monsignor H. A. Buchholtz, P.A., Rector, St. Peter's Cathedral; July 17, 1936.

[13] Personal Correspondence between Archie J. Verville, General Building Construction, and A. O. Pechaeur, c/o Harrigan Gas & Oil Co., Bank Building, Marquette, Mich.; July 24, 1936.

14 Personal Correspondence between Edward A. Schilling, Architect, and
        A. O. Pechaeur, July 27, 1936.

15 Personal Correspondence between Archie J. Verville, General Building
        Construction, and Monsignor H. A. Buchholtz, P.A., Rector,
        St. Peter's Cathedral, Sept. 2, 1936.

16 Personal Correspondence between Archie J. Verville, General Building
        Construction, and A. O. Pechaeur, Sept. 7, 1936.

17 Final Billing Statement from Archie J. Verville, General Building
        Construction; Sept. 7, 1936.

18 Personal Correspondence between George Powrie, Detroit, Mich. and
        Edward A. Schilling, Architect; May 22, 1936.

19 "ibid".

20 "ibid".

21 Time Sheets from George Powrie, Detroit, Mich; 1936.

22 "Op. Cit." The Marquette Mining Journal, August, 1936.

23 Request for Payment from The Hutter Construction Company, 134 Western
        Ave., Fond du Lac, Wisc.; to St. Peter's Cathedral, Marquette,
        Mich.; August, 24, 1936.

24 General Contractor Specifications from Edward A. Schilling, Architect,
        to Monsignor H. A. Buchholtz, P.A., Rector, St. Peter's Cathedral.

25 Detailed Estimate from Levine Bros., Heating & Plumbing, 219 W. Washington
        St., Marquette, Mich., to Monsignor H. A. Buchholtz, P.A., Rector,
        St. Peter's Cathedral.

26 Personal Correspondence between H. J. Runnings, Mechanical Engineer, Levine
        Bros., Heating & Plumbing, and Edward A. Schilling, Architect;
        August 16, 1936.

27 Personal Correspondence between Isidore Diebold, O.S.B., St. Mary's Church,
        Maryville, Mo. and Edward A. Schilling, Architect; April 10, 1935.

28 Personal Correspondence between T. Werth, St. Bernard's Church, Thief
River Falls, Minn., and Edward A. Schilling, Architect; Sept. 6, 1935.

29 Personal Correspondence between E. J. Lusiere, St. Joseph's Church, Rid
Lake Falls, Minn., and Edward A. Schilling, Architect; Sept. 10, 1935.

30 Personal Correspondence between Rev. Henry D. Paneiz, Olivia, Minn.,
and Edward A. Schilling, Architect; Dec. 11, 1935.

31 Personal Correspondence between Frank Bruce, Milwaukee, Wisc., and
Edward, A. Schilling, Architect; Aug. 17, 1936.

32 Contract between V & M Electric Co., Menominee, Mich., and Bishop
Joseph C. Plagens, D.D., Diocese of Sault Ste. Marie and Marquette,
Mich.; Aug. 1, 1936.

33 Contract between Detroit Mantel and Tile Co., Lighting & Fixtures, 1431
Farmer St., Detroit, Mich., and Bishop Joseph C. Plagens, D.D.,
Diocese of Sault Ste. Marie & Marquette, Mich..

34 Personal Correspondence between Monsignor H. A. Buchholtz, P.A., Rector
St. Peter's Cathedral, and the Hutter Construction Co.; Aug. 17, 1936.

35 Personal Correspondence between The Hutter Construction Co., and Edward
A. Schilling, Architect; Oct. 5, 1936.

36 Personal Correspondence between The Hutter Construction Co., and Monsignor
H. A. Buchholtz, P.A., Rector, St. Peter's Cathedral; March 1, 1937.

37 Personal Correspondence between The Hutter Construction Co., and Edward
A. Schilling, Architect; Sept. 11, 1936.

38 Personal Correspondence between Edward A. Schilling, Architect, and
Monsignor H. A. Buchholtz, P.A., Rector, St. Peter's Cathedral,
Sept. 14, 1936.

39 Personal Correspondence between The Hutter Construction Co., and Bishop
Joseph C. Plagens, D.D., Diocese of Sault Ste. Marie and Marquette,
Mich.; Aug. 1, 1936.

40 Personal Correspondence between The Hutter Construction Co., and Edward
A. Schilling, Architect; Oct. 1, 1936.

41 Personal Correspondence between The Hutter Construction Co., and Bishop
        Joseph C. Plagens, D.D., Diocese of Sault Ste. Marie and Marquette,
        Mich.; Nov. 3, 1936.

42 Personal Correspondence between The Hutter Construction Co., and Edward
        A. Schilling, Architect; May 14, 1937.

43 "Op. Cit." Hutter and Plagens; Nov. 3, 1936.

44 Personal Correspondence between Monsignor H. A. Buchholtz, P.A., Rector,
        St. Peter's Cathedral, and Edward A. Schilling, Architect; June 16, 1936.

45 Personal Correspondence between Edward A. Schilling, Architect, and Monsignor
        H. A. Buchholtz, P.A., Rector, St. Peter's Cathedral; May 27, 1936.

46 Personal Correspondence between The Hutter Construction Company and
        Monsignor H. A. Buchholtz, P.A., Rector, St. Peter's Cathedral;
        Aug. 25, 1936.

47 Personal Correspondence between The Hutter Construction Co., and Monsignor
        H. A. Buchholtz, P.A., Rector, St. Peter's Cathedral; July 24, 1939.

48 Personal Correspondence between The Hutter Construction Co., and Monsignor
        H. A. Buchholtz, P.A., Rector, St. Peter's Cathedral; July 12, 1939.

49 Personal Correspondence between Edward A. Schilling, Architect, and
        Monsignor H. A. Buchholtz, P.A., Rector, St. Peter's Cathedral;
        Feb. 2, 1937.

50 "ibid".

51 Personal Correspondence between Mr. Rock Beauchamp, 409 S. Fourth St.,
        Marquette, Mich., and Edward A. Schilling, Architect: Aug. 2, 1938.

52 Personal Correspondence between The Hutter Construction Co., and Bishop
        Joseph C. Plagens, D.D., Sault Ste. Marie and Marquette, Mich.;
        Feb. 9, 1937.

53 Personal Correspondence between George F. Hutter, The Hutter Construction
        Co., and Monsignor H. A. Buchholtz, P.A., Rector, St. Peter's
        Cathedral: Nov. 16, 1937.

54 Personal Corresponcence between E. Stroethner, T.C. Esser Co., 3107 W.
        Galena St., Milwaukee, Wisc., and Monsignor H. A. Buchholtz, P.A.,
        Rector, St. Peter's Cathedral: March 12, 1937.

55 Personal Correspondence between E. Stroethner, T.C. Esser Co., and Monsignor
   H. A. Buchholtz, P.A., Rector, St. Peter's Cathedral; April 24, 1937.

56 Personal Correspondence between Edward A. Schilling, Architect, and Bishop
   Joseph C. Plagens, D.D., Diocese of Sault Ste. Marie and Marquette,
   Mich.; April 20, 1937.

57 Personal Correspondence between Edward A. Schilling, Architect, "Specifications
   for Art Glass Windows For St. Peter's Cathedral, Marquette, Mich.",
   and Bishop Joseph C. Plagens, D.D., Diocese of Sault Ste. Marie and
   Marquette, Mich.; May, 1937.

58 Personal Correspondence between Detroit Stained Glass Works, 4831-4833
   Fort St., West, Detroit, Mich., and Bishop Joseph C. Plagens, D.D.,
   Diocese of Sault Ste. Marie and Marquette, Mich., Monsignor H. A.
   Buchholtz, P.A., Rector, St. Peter's Cathedral, and Edward A.
   Schilling, Architect; May 28, 1937.

59 "Art Glass Window contract; ST. Peter's Cathedral, Marquette, Mich.";
   between Bishop Joseph C. Plagens, D.D., Diocese of Sault Ste.
   Marie and Marquette, Mich., Monsignor H. A. Buchholtz, P.A.,
   Rector, St. Peter's Cathedral, and Detroit Stained Glass Works:
   July 28, 1937.

60 Personal Correspondence between Edward A. Schilling, Architect, "Pew
   Specification For St. Peter's Cathedral, Marquette, Mich.";
   and Monsignor H. A. Buchholtz, P.A., Rector, St. Peter's Cathedral;
   Sept., 1936.

61 Contract between American Seating Co., Grand Rapids, Mich., and Bishop
   Joseph C. Plagens, D.D., Diocese of Sault Ste. Marie and Marquette,
   Mich.; Oct. 23, 1936.

62 Correspondence from American Seating Co., to Mr. N. J. Dobson, U.P.
   Office Supply Co., Marquette, Mich.; Oct. 29, 1936.

63 Personal Correspondence between Edward A. Schilling, Architect, and
   Monsignor H. A. Buchholtz, P.A., Rector, St. Peter's Cathedral;
   March 11, 1938.

64 Personal Correspondence between The Hutter Construction Co., and American
   Seating Co.; January 31, 1938.

65 Personal Correspondence between The International Statuary and Altar Co.,
   Milwaukee, Wisc., "Specifications of Proposed Altar and Shrines
   For St. Peter's Cathedral, Marquette, Mich." and Monsignor H. A.
   Buchholtz, P.A., Rector, ST. Peter's Cathedral; June 9, 1937.

66 Personal Correspondence between The International Statuary and Altar Co.,
        and Monsignor H. A. Buchholtz, P.A., Rector, St. Peter's Cathedral;
        Aug. 9, 1937.

67 Personal Correspondence between The International Statuary and Altar Co.,
        and Monsignor H. A. Buchholtz, P.A., Rector, St. Peter's Cathedral;
        Oct. 29, 1937.

68 Personal Correspondence between Mrs. Eva Moroder, representing The
        International Statuary and Altar Co., and Edward A. Schilling,
        Architect; Feb. 14, 1938.

69 Personal Correspondence between Guiseppe Tommassi Studios, Ecclesiastical
        Art Marble Specialists, Pietrasanta, Carrara (Italy), New York,
        and Chicago; 25 East Delaware Place, Chicago, Ill., and Bishop
        Joseph C. Plagens, D.D., Diocese of Sault Ste. Marie and Marquette,
        Mich.; November 2, 1937.

70 Personal Correspondence between Guiseppe Tommasi Studios, and Monsignor
        H. A. Buchholtz, P.A., Rector, St. Peter's Cathedral; Feb. 21, 1938.

71 Contract between Guiseppe Tommasi Studios, and Bishop Joseph C. Plagens,
        D.D., Diocese of Sault Ste. Marie and Marquette, Mich.; March 13,1938.

72 Personal Correspondence between Guiseppe Tommasi Studios, and Monsignor
        H. A. Buchholtz, P.A., Rector, St. Peter's Cathedral; April 12, 1938.

73 "ibid".

74 "ibid".

75 Personal Correspondence between Guiseppe Tommasi Studios, and Monsignor
        H. A. Buchholtz, P.A., Rector, St. Peter's Cathedral; May 16, 1938.

76 Personal Correspondence between Guiseppe Tommasi Studios, and Monsignor
        H. A. Buchholtz, P.A., Rector, ST. Peter's Cathedral; Feb. 25, 1938.

77 Personal Correspondence between The International Statuary and Altar Co.,
        Milwaukee, Wisc., and Monsignor H. A. Buchholtz, P.A., Rector,
        St. Peter's Cathedral; Oct. 5, 1937.

78 Contract between The Tiffin Manufacturing Co., Tiffin, Ohio, and Bishop
        Joseph C. Plagens, D.D., Diocese of Sault Ste. Marie and Marquette,
        Mich.; June 25, 1938.

[79] Personal Correspondence between The Tiffin Manufacturing Co., and Monsignor H. A. Buchholtz, P.A., Rector, St. Peter's Cathedral: June 2, 1938.

[80] Personal Correspondence between The Tiffin Manufacturing Co., and Edward A. Schilling, Architect: December 30, 1938.

[81] Personal Correspondence between Karl Hackert, Church Interiors, 840 North Michigan Ave., Chicago, Ill., and Monsignor H. A. Buchholtz, P.A., Rector, St. Peter's Cathedral; January 16, 1941.

[82] Contract between Karl Hackert, Church Interiors, 215 West Ohio St., Chicago, Ill., and Bishop Thomas L. Hoa, D.D., Diocese of Sault Ste. Marie and Marquette, Mich.; September 27, 1947.

[83] "ibid".

[84] "ibid".

[85] Personal Correspondence between Karl Hackert, Church Interiors, and Monsignor John T. Holland, Rector, St. Peter's Cathedral; March 9, 1948.

[86] Personal Correspondence between Karl Hackert, Church Interiors, and Monsignor John T. Holland, Rector, St. Peter's Cathedral; May 18, 1948.

[87] Cappo, Rev. Louis C., Personal Communication.

[88] Pepin, Rev. Darryl J., Personal Communication.

[89] "Op. Cit." The Mining Journal; Tuesday, May 10, 1949.

[90] "Op. Cit." Our Sunday Visitor; August 30, 1953.

[91] The Mining Journal; "New Stained Glass windows Are Installed In Cathedral", Marquette, Mich.; February 19, 1938.

[92] Rupp, Rev. Daniel, Personal Communication.

ACKNOWLEDGEMENTS

I would like to formally thank those individuals who were helpful in the preparation of this book.

Dr. Barry Knight, Professor of History at NMU for his guidance, patience and understanding as the director of the initial project.

Monsignor Louis Cappo, Fr. Ronald Skufca and the staff of St. Peter's Cathedral for their help and encouragement.

Monsignor Nolan B. McKevitt for reference materials and cooperation.

Members of the administration and staff of the Diocese of Marquette for their help and encouragement and especially to Mr. Greg Bell.

Ms. Dawn Betts for her help in the typing and retyping of this paper.

To my wife, Claudia, and my children Jeff, Jody, Jayme, and Jillian without whose patience and love, I would have given up on this project many months ago.

To those who helped with the revisions and publication of this book, including Deacon Thomas Foye and his wife Denise, and the Bishop Baraga Association, with special thanks to Len McKeen, Carley Challender, and Carmen Hammes.

And finally, the Holy Spirit, without whom this could not have been possible.